GREAT SOUTH AFRICAN CHRISTIANS

Great
South African
Christians

by

HORTON DAVIES

GEOFFREY CUMBERLEGE
OXFORD UNIVERSITY PRESS
Cape Town   London   New York
1951

Oxford University Press, Amen House, London, E.C.4

GLASGOW   NEW YORK   TORONTO   MELBOURNE
WELLINGTON   BOMBAY   CALCUTTA   MADRAS   CAPE TOWN

Geoffrey Cumberlege, Publisher to the University

❧ PRINTED IN SOUTH AFRICA BY
THE RUSTICA PRESS, LTD., WYNBERG, CAPE.

To

D.M.D.

Minister of the Word of God
and my father

ACKNOWLEDGEMENTS

My main obligations to authors, volumes and publishers are listed in the Select Bibliography, but this opportunity is afforded of thanking the Epworth Press for permission to cite from Edwin W. Smith's *The Life and Times of Daniel Lindley*, 1801-1890, and Messrs. Hodder & Stoughton for permission to cite from C. F. Andrews's *John White of Mashonaland*. Dr. Edwin W. Smith has been good enough to read the MS. and to improve it by several corrections and suggestions drawn from his wide and deep knowledge of the history of Christian Missions in Southern Africa. It is also a pleasure to thank my colleagues, Professor C. D. Hérisson and the Rev. L. A. Hewson, for reading the proofs, and one of my students, Mr. D. R. Briggs, B.A., for compiling the Index.

Most of the ensuing Chapters, though since revised, appeared as articles in *The Outspan* and are reprinted by the courtesy of Mr. Gordon Makepeace, the Editor.

H.D.

Rhodes University,
   Grahamstown,
      Whitsuntide, 1951

CONTENTS

INTRODUCTION

THE PRINCIPLES OF SELECTION

IN the series entitled GREAT SOUTH AFRICAN CHRISTIANS a choice of eighteen representative Christian leaders has been made ranging over a period of two hundred and fifty years, from Georg Schmidt who was born in 1709 to the Rev. John White who died as recently as 1933. In a sense the writer did not choose them; they chose themselves. That is, they were already distinguished in their lifetime and they have lived on in the history of South Africa and are evergreen in the annals of the Church. If their memory deserved to survive, their closest friends and admirers refused to allow the remembrance of them to be buried in their graves but resurrected them in biographies. In that sense, too, they were already candidates for selection in such a series. They being dead, yet speak. Their biographies are, in Milton's words ' the precious life-blood of a master spirit '.

Yet it would be wrong to conclude that there was no other principle of selection at work, although the primary sortation had already been made. There are several distinguished South African Christians whose memories have been embalmed in memoirs. There are, it must be confessed, many notable absentees in this series. A pioneer missionary such as Charles Brownlee of Kingwilliamstown had to give way to earlier pioneers. A woman of distinction, Christina Forsyth of Fingoland, ceded the palm to Mother Cecile because of the latter's distinctive educational importance as foundress of the Grahamstown Training College. An African minister such as Tiyo Soga was omitted in favour of the Christian Chief of the

Bamangwato of Bechuanaland, Khama, because the latter was a layman and a responsible ruler. All that needs to be stated is that it is not claimed that those included in this series of sketches were greater Christians than those who were excluded. The reader may supplement this gallery with his own favourite snapshots, for there are many great Christians who were almost anonymous, as the Church remembers in its great festival of All Souls.

All candidates for Christian greatness now living were excluded, because comparisons are invidious, if not embarrassing. Though it is far from our meaning to imply that the only good and great South African Christians are dead ones! How could this be when we have living among us diverse examples of Christian greatness? We have Michael Scott, a prophet with an eye for injustice as acute as Amos and as compassionate as Hosea. There is Alan Paton who has preached one of the most sublime sermons in our time on the text ' Thou shalt love thy neighbour as thyself' in his soul-stirring book *Cry, the Beloved Country*. Nor must we forget Professor J. D. du Toit ('Totius'), who has written Christian paraphrases of the Psalms which bid fair to live as long in the Afrikaans language as those of Isaac Watts in the English tongue.

Not only the living, but also controversial figures were excluded from our selection. Men as different as Paul Kruger and J. H. Hofmeyr, Bishop Colenso and Professor J. D. du Plessis, would have made good their claim but for the smoke of political and ecclesiastical warfare which still obscures the profiles of their greatness. Since this series aims at evoking admiration and imitation, it would fail entirely if it led instead to argumentation and recrimination.

Those figures chosen had to be, in a word, *representative*. They were selected to illustrate three types of variety amongst outstanding Christians on the South

African scene. In the first place they represent *variety of nationality*; in the second place, they represent *differences of Christian allegiance*, of denomination; and, in the third place, they represent *diversities of Christian service*.

In this series, then, a whole range of nationalities is disclosed. First, we notice the remarkable contribution made by the Scots of whom five sketches are included. Their names are: Livingstone, Moffat, Shaw, Philip and Stewart and they bear a family likeness. Each is inviolably independent in outlook, each a champion of the under-privileged, and each an ambitious strategist for the Kingdom of God. Three are English, Bishop Gray, Mother Cecile and John White. There are two Germans: Pfanner and Schmidt, men of zeal and determination. France owns Casalis and Coillard, while Switzerland claims Creux and Berthoud, compounded of the sensitivity and wit of those nations. South Africa rejoices that Andrew Murray and Stefanus Hofmeyr were born here. Three nations have one representative each: the U.S.A. own Lindley, the Bantu boast of Khama who, as a Chief, pioneered the journey from heathenism to Christianity, and Holland and Judaism lay joint claim to the parentage of the poet-pastor Jan Lion Cachet.

There is an equally wide denominational representation. The lead is taken by the Reformed Churches (Dutch, Swiss, French and Scottish) which have seven claimants to fame. Next come the Congregationalists with three (all servants of the London Missionary Society). In addition there are two Anglicans, two Methodists, one Roman Catholic and one Moravian. As many nationalities bring their common tribute to Our Lord, so do many Christian Communions.

The great South African Christians display astonishing diversities of gifts. Some of them were creative minds who dreamed dreams of greatness for their Church.

Robert Gray, for example, came to the Cape to found one diocese and died bequeathing six to the future. Schmidt founded the first industrial and educational missionary settlement at Genadendal; scores of similar settlements and institutions were founded in other Communions by imitation, including Lovedale, Healdtown, and Mariann-hill. Shaw's vision of a chain of mission stations from Salem to Natal was realized in his own lifetime, but the fulfilment of this promise is only known to-day in the Methodist African harvest, greater than that of any other South African Communion. Abbot Pfanner of Mariann-hill began by modifying the strict Trappist discipline to permit members of the Order to become missionaries; in the end the change was so revolutionary and far-reaching that the Holy See recognized it as a new Congregation with its own rules and distinctive dress.

Others, again, were the first to apply old ideas in a new country. They were pioneers who endured the dangers and discomforts of wild animals and savages for the sake of the Gospel of Christ. Of such were Creux and Berthoud in the northern Transvaal, Coillard in Barotseland, Casalis in Basutoland, and Livingstone throughout Central Africa. The story of Creux's sacrifices (his wife and all his children were buried on missionary ground) and of Coillard's heroic perseverance in the face of failure are only two outstanding examples of Christian courage.

Yet others were notable champions of the under-privileged Coloured and African people, enduring persecution and criticism for Christ's sake. Of these, indeed, the contemporary world was not worthy. This goodly succession of prophets included Philip and Livingstone, Moffat and White. They deserved to be called ' the custodians of South Africa's conscience '.

Still others were remarkable for their many-sided aptitudes and accomplishments. Men of great versatility were: Livingstone (medical missionary, scientist and explorer), Andrew Murray (preacher, administrator, author and educationalist), Stewart (Doctor of Divinity and Doctor of Medicine), J. Lion Cachet (predikant, professor and poet), and Abbot Pfanner (like Mother Cecile an ascetic, an administrator and an educationalist).

The variety and importance of this contribution to the Christianizing and civilizing of South Africa may readily be realized in one single field, the educational. Eliminate the example and influence of Robert Gray and Andrew Murray, and we should be without the University of the Orange Free State and Huguenot University College, not to mention the great Anglican private schools such as Bishop's, and St. Andrew's, Grahamstown, and St. John's Johannesburg, to name only the boys' schools, and ignoring all the other educational foundations of other Communions. Remove the missionary influence from education and it is doubtful if Native education in any form would exist to-day, much less its apex, the South African Native College at Fort Hare. Above all, remove the influence of Christians, ministerial or lay, and the history of South Africa might continue to be a never-ending series of Kaffir Wars. An enduring civilization cannot be built upon the shifting sands of frontier conditions. The ambassadors of Christ, far from ' meddling with the Natives ' have, in fact, helped to resolve the inter-racial tensions, apart from which reconciliation an enduring civilization in Africa could not have been built.

There may still be two unanswered questions in the mind of the reader. First, how do you define the term ' South African '? Second, how do you define ' greatness ' or ' Christian greatness '? The first can be answered briefly. The term ' South African ' is used in its widest possible connotation, to mean any distinguished person whose name is associated with South Africa, or who lived for a considerable part of his working life in South Africa.

The second question is more difficult to answer, for greatness is an attribute or series of attributes that it is easier to recognize than to define. The same is true of great art as of great music. But the writer would suggest that the epithet of ' great ' as applied to Christians should be withheld unless the claimant incarnates in varying degrees four dominant Christian qualities. The candidate must be a man (or woman) of invincible faith and, therefore, of courage; a man of infinite compassion (annihilating all distinctions of class or creed or pigmentation), and be as humble as only God's greatest servants are. Great Christians, in the writer's view, must be faithful, fearless, compassionate and humble. Of the first characteristic Coillard is the outstanding example, of the second Livingstone, of the third Creux or van der Kemp, and of the fourth (perhaps the most difficult, attainable only in the kneeling position) Andrew Murray.

The only danger of such a series is that it may incline readers to think these are plaster-saints, haloed and inimitable figures of the past with no contemporary message. Saints, it cannot be said too often, are not born, but made. And toil, struggle, sweat and holy tears go into the crucible of their creation. In the affairs of the world some are indeed born great — in the world of the spirit all have to attain greatness.

Moreover, some of the most handicapped in the race of the Spirit have breasted the tape. The miracle of the dissolute Augustine who became a saint was re-enacted in the life of Hofmeyr. The overworked and underpaid gardener became, by another miracle, Robert Moffat, Freeman of the Cities of London and Glasgow. The sick boy expected to die of tuberculosis becomes, in the providence of God, Gray, the founder of the Church of the Province. The gaol-bird, Georg Schmidt, through the calling of God, becomes the historic pioneer of missions in Southern Africa. The Jew brought up in the slums of Amsterdam becomes, under Divine guidance, a renowned predikant and poet, as Dominus Jan Lion Cachet. The American boy who excels at shooting squirrels is transformed, by the sculpture of the Divine Artist, into the first minister of the Voortrekkers. With God only the unexpected happens!

In brief, the pre-eminence of these Christians is due to their obedience. They are simple soldiers who take the marching orders of the Word of God as their iron-ration. While others among us hesitate, delay or compromise, they obey. As François Coillard so often repeated, ' Obedience is the politeness of the soldier.'

These portraits are, then, glimpses of the Acts of the Apostles in South Africa. They present a saga of Christian service to God and man that is not closed, but continuing. They illustrate the greatness that is possible to men. The point of contact between the heroes of yesterday and the demands of to-day is provided in the penetrating saying of G. K. Chesterton: ' Religion makes the ordinary man extraordinary'.

South African needs extraordinary men, which is simply another way of saying that she needs Christians. These portraits show us Christians in action.

CHAPTER I

GEORG SCHMIDT

ON 9 July, 1737, Georg Schmidt, a German, arrived in Cape Town. It was a historic event, though the citizens of Cape Town thought it a laughing-matter, for he was the first Protestant missionary to reach the shores of Southern Africa. Aged 28, he was born in Moravia and had joined the Herrnhut Community of Brethren founded by that great servant of God, Count Zinzendorf in Silesia. He returned to the land of his birth, where Protestantism was persecuted, and he and his companion, Melchior Nitschmann, were thrown into gaol. There they suffered great indignities. Heavily manacled, they were made to perform the most degrading duties, and, when exhaustion slowed up their efforts, they were speeded up by kicks and blows. Their only sustenance was bread and water, and at night they were thrust into ice-cold and clammy cells. The brutal treatment killed the senior man, but Schmidt lived on for six long and almost unbearable years. Of indomitable faith, he declared, ' I cried to my Saviour and He made it so that I did not feel the cold so much.'

In 1734 he was released and returned to Herrnhut, where the Brothers had established a family community life in Christ. This was that rare achievement — a family monasticism. The members of the Community were withdrawn from the world, but they did not practise asceticism. Each man and woman fulfilled his or her vocation (smith, carpenter, laundress) to the glory of God and the communal good. The Christocracy of this Community was symbolized by the central prayer-hall with its high belfry.

1

On the representation of two Dutch Reformed Ministers of the Amsterdam Classis the Moravian Brethren of Herrnhut were invited to send a missionary to evangelize the South African Hottentots. Schmidt was selected and he came alone (although it was the custom of the Brothers to send out missionaries in twos or threes). Happily for him, the future was veiled in secrecy, and he could not forecast that, as he had been persecuted by Catholics, so would he be prevented from continuing his work through the jealous vested interests of the Protestants in the Cape.

In Cape Town he was ridiculed, as if his object — evangelizing the Hottentots — was fantastically foolish. The Hottentots were thought by many to be beyond redemption. However, Schmidt had the Governor's approval and a military corporal to escort him. In this manner he travelled to the interior. About a hundred miles from Cape Town he crossed the Zondereind River and settled first at Hartebeest Kraal on the edge of the habitat of the Hottentots. Here he remained for the most part of a year. We get a glimpse into his methods from his journal. He wrote:

> Every evening I visited the Hottentots, sat down among them, distributed tobacco, and began to smoke with them. I told them that, moved by sincere love, I had come to them to make them acquainted with their Saviour and to assist them to work. Upon this Afrika replied: ' That is good, Baas.' I asked them if they knew that there was a great Baas, who had given them their cattle and all they possessed. ' Yes,' answered Afrika. ' What do you call him?' ' We call him Tui'qua,' was the reply. Thereupon I rejoined, ' Oh, dear people, this Tui'qua is our Saviour; He became man, and for us men He died upon the cross!'

In 1738 Schmidt removed his mission to Baviaan's Kloof (the Dale of Baboons). He took eighteen Hottentots with him and it was hard work. They did not understand why a man should come among them to talk about God. Now if he had come to trade that would have been intelligible! Some gathered around him for the daily prayers, but soon their curiosity was expended. The missionary became dejected, ill and lonely. His one consolation was the knowledge that five of his catechumens were worthy of baptism and entry into the membership of the Church. He therefore wrote to Count Zinzendorf for a certificate of ordination, that he might administer baptism to the converts. On receiving it, he baptized the five Hottentots, giving them the Christian names of Josua, Christian, Jonas, Christina and Magdalena. The Dutch Reformed Church in the Colony, fearing that this constituted the creation of a new denomination in the Cape and, therefore, an infringement of their ecclesiastical monopoly, urged the Council of Seventeen to demand his recall. This action was taken, despite the fact that it was at the request of the Amsterdam Presbytery of this great Church that Schmidt had come out to the Cape. There was nothing for it but Schmidt's return in 1744. And this, by all human calculations, meant the end of the work at Baviaan's Kloof, renamed Genadendal (the Glen of Grace).

Schmidt left with a sad heart, and had to be satisfied with Governor Swellengrebel's promise that the Hottentots would be allowed to remain in residence at Baviaan's Kloof under official government protection. On his return to Europe the missionary continued his evangelical labours in various parts of Moravia, Silesia and Bohemia. The evening of his life was spent in Niesky, where he died in 1785 at the age of seventy-six. He was throughout his life a man of faith, of prayer and of abundant charitable works. It was his joy from time to time to hear news of his beloved Hottentots.

What had he left in the Glen of Grace? There were five converts, a few seekers after the Christian truth, a garden, a pear-tree he had planted, and the Dutch New

Testament which he had placed in the hands of Magdalena. Soon, by all human predictions, the house would disintegrate and creeper would cover the pear-tree and the garden; the creeper of apathy would strangle the faith of the neophytes, and the New Testament would be used for the tinder of a hut fire. Man guesses, but God governs!

In 1792, almost fifty years after Schmidt left his unfinished task, the authorities at the Cape were more propitious, and three Moravian missionaries came to the Glen of Grace to continue Schmidt's work. They were Hendrik Marsveld, a Hollander, Daniel Schwinn and Johann Christian Kühnel, Germans, aged respectively, 47, 42 and 30. They were unmarried and each had been apprenticed to a trade and afterwards ordained as deacons of the *Unitas Fratrum* (The United Brethren). They expected to find no traces of their predecessor's work, but they discovered the ruined house of Schmidt, traced the outlines of his garden and orchard, and found the pear-tree flourishing. They asked the Hottentots if anyone remembered the missionary who had left half a century before. To their surprise they were told to visit a hut in which an old woman lived. The old lady, now almost blind, said, ' *Mynheer* Schmidt baptized me and gave me the name of Magdalena.' She then fumbled in the corner of her hut, pulled out a couple of sheepskins and disclosed a leather bag within, and inside that was the Dutch New Testament that Schmidt had given her. They asked her if she could read it, but she pointed her grand-daughter out to them. The latter had been taught to read by a pupil of Schmidt's and she read out to them the second chapter of St. Matthew's Gospel. Thus, in a most marvellous way, the missionary had been withdrawn, but the Word of God had continued to be read.

The new missionaries built a station, a school, a mill and a cutlery. In the latter they made pruning-knives which were in great demand by the fruit-farmers of the district who called them *herrnhuters*. The Brethren found a ruin and established a thriving manufacturing village where all labour was dedicated to God.

Lady Anne Barnard, who visited Genadendal in 1798, was deeply impressed by all she saw. Of the moving service which she attended she writes:

> Presently the Church bell was a-ringing and we begged leave to make part of the congregation. I doubt much whether I should have entered St. Peter's at Rome, with the triple crown, with a more devout impression of the Deity and His Presence than I felt in this little church of a few feet square, where the simple disciples of Christianity, dressed in the skins of animals, knew no purple or fine linen, no pride or hypocrisy. I felt as if I were creeping back 1700 years, and heard, from the rude and inspired lips of Evangelists, the simple sacred words of wisdom and purity.

Lady Anne then goes on to describe the worship in detail:

> The service began with a Presbyterian form of psalm; about 150 Hottentots joined in the twenty-third psalm in a tone so sweet and loud, so chaste and true, that is was impossible to hear it without being surprised. The fathers, who were the sole music-masters, sang in their deep-toned bass along with them and the harmony was excellent. This over, the miller took a portion of the Scripture and expounded it as he went along. The father's discourse was short, and his voice was even and natural, and when he used the words, as he often did, *Mijne lieve vrienden* ('My beloved friends') I felt that he thought they were all his children.

A hundred years after Schmidt's arrival a young French missionary stayed at Genadendal on his way from Basuto-land to his future wife in Cape Town. Eugène Casalis (for that was his name) passed through early in 1836 and was enthralled by all that he saw. He noted a square in the middle of which stood a vast cruciform church, surmounted by a high belfry. Surrounding the square were the homes of six or seven missionary families, and adjacent were the six lodges in which travellers were housed for the night. As he entered the Glen of Grace he saw the neat cottages in which the Hottentots lived on either side of him.

He was housed in one of the cool apartments set aside for visitors, in which there was a bed, a table covered with linen and on it a Bible, a few chairs, and a washstand in which Casalis dipped his travel-stained head several times. A Hottentot woman brought him peaches, grapes, bread and a cup of coffee. When a bell sounded, he entered the common refectory where the missionary brothers and sisters ate. He was seated next to the Director, Bishop Teusch, who later conducted him round the entire station. Casalis remarked on the simplicity and friendliness of the missionaries, each of whom shook hands with him. He was also interested in their unusual dress. The men wore flat, long-peaked caps, blue overalls, and supple sheepskin trousers, very like chamois in texture. The women had high, twisted black bonnets and long, flowing cotton dresses. The meal ended, the Bishop showed him round the three schools, all of which were taught by Hottentot masters and mistresses; the workshops of the smiths, wagon-makers, cutlers, carpenters, laundresses, and the water-mill. He traversed the allotments, orchards and grain-fields that had to cater for the two thousand members of the community. (It had only numbered three hundred in Lady Anne's time, forty years before.) The French missionary noted with appreciation that the skilled work was all done by Hottentots, the Brothers only serving in an advisory capacity. He learned that here was practised a simple Christian Communism, where all the profits were shared among the workers. He was then taken to view the cemetery where Hottentots and missionaries were buried, as they had laboured, together.

As evening came on, a bell summoned to prayers and they went into the huge church which accommodated 2,000 persons. A Hottentot played the organ and a Moravian Brother conducted the simple family service. At the conclusion of the service each person shook his neighbour's hand and said, *Slaap gerust*! Casalis's tribute is best ended in his own felicitous phrasing:

I, too, slept in peace, my body tired out by the morning's ride, but my soul sweetly cradled by the holy memories of the afternoon. I devoted the next day's work to studying in more detail the wholesome and touching customs of this Christian beehive. Then I left, recalling the words recently spoken by an English Colonel, ' Truly, if these Moravian Brethren would consent, I would beg them to let me retire in their midst.'

Another hundred years goes by and this time Dr. R. H. W. Shepherd, the present Principal of Lovedale, records his impressions of Genadendal as he saw it when he was present in 1937 at the bicentenary celebrations of Schmidt's landing. These impressions are contained in a series of fascinating vignettes of South African missionary life, entitled *Where Aloes Flame*. He remarks on the great change in the official attitude towards Genadendal that has taken place in two hundred years. Schmidt was officially requested to leave the Cape, but his successors were greeted in an official letter from His Excellency the Governor-General congratulating them on two centuries of evangelistic and educational zeal. Impressive as the official services were, with hundreds unable to gain admission to the vast church, Dr. Shepherd writes:

Even more moving was it when after service a group of missionaries stood in a book-lined room and from a box made out of the wood of the pear-tree Georg Schmidt planted, there was taken a Testament hoary with age. It was the book Schmidt gave to Lena (Magdalena) before he went away. The gulf of the years vanished as one took into one's hand what had rested in Georg Schmidt's own and also Lena's.

The faith of Schmidt has been splendidly vindicated, and, on the site of his house a great boulder now stands, bearing the inscription:

Georg Schmidt
Die eerste Evangeliese
Sendeling in Suid-Afrika
Gebore 30 September 1709 te Kunewalde in Morawie
Werktyd in Suid-Afrika 9 Julie 1737 tot 5 Maart 1744
Oorlede 1 Augustus 1785 te Niesky in Duitsland.

Underneath is a most appropriate quotation from Psalm 126, verse 5: 'Those that sow in tears shall reap in joy.'

Thus South Africa's first Protestant missionary is fittingly celebrated and the celebration is itself proof that the seed of the Gospel flourishes secretly, if prohibited openly, and that the Risen Christ is perpetually breaking forth from the sepulchre of the sceptics. There is a poetic justice in concluding with a sincere tribute from the leader of the Church which once asked Schmidt to leave. The words are Dr. Andrew Murray's: ' There was in the Brethren first of all that detachment from the world and its hopes, that power of endurance, that simple trust in God, which affliction and persecution are meant to work. These men were literally strangers and pilgrims on the earth.'

These ' strangers and pilgrims ' have become the friends and benefactors of South Africa, making the wilderness of arid race-relations blossom like the rose, and transforming the ' Dale of Baboons ' into the ' Glen of Grace '.

CHAPTER II

JOHN PHILIP

DR. JOHN PHILIP proves the truth of the adage that a prophet is honoured, except in his own country. Although he was acclaimed in England as the 'Wilberforce of Africa' for his championship of the Coloured peoples, yet Sir Lowry Cole spoke the verdict of South Africans when he described Philip as 'more of a politician than a missionary'. Philip's character and reputation are enigmatic. This may be seen by comparing the eulogy of his memorial tablet in the oldest Congregational Church in Cape Town with the detraction of Lord Charles Somerset. The memorial tablet (marble is an exaggerator, admittedly) lauds him 'as one whose intellect was consecrated to the service of Divine truth . . . whose life was faithfully spent for the glory of God in the welfare of man', and adds that his residence of thirty years in Cape Town caused him to be 'known as an unflinching advocate of Christian missions, an unwearied friend of the oppressed, and an able preacher . . .'. With this may be contrasted Somerset's references in a letter to the English Secretary of State to 'the insidiousness of this dangerous man's character' and to 'his mingling himself in everything that could give him political importance'.

Clearly, Philip was a man of dominating personality and iron determination; in fact, an Independent of the Independents, who, like the Puritans, feared God and therefore feared no one else. This stormy petrel dominated the South African political and religious landscape for thirty years. Men might praise him, or more frequently abuse him: what they could not do was ignore him.

9

His name is commemorated in the town of Philippolis (literally ' Philip's city '), and in every history of South Africa (whether the estimates are unfavourable as in G. M. Theal and Sir George Cory, or favourable as in W. M. Macmillan). Most unexpectedly, perhaps, he emerges as the first and most thorough advocate of segregation, which he approved as a safeguard for the Coloured and African people. He presents one of the most controversial and fascinating character-studies in South African history.

John Philip was born in Kirkcaldy, Fife, in 1775, and in his early teens re-echoed, as did every poor man's son, the watchword of the French Revolution, ' Liberty, Equality and Fraternity '. His father was a weaver in the days before the Industrial Revolution with its ' dark, Satanic mills ', and then every man worked with dignity and independence in his own home. The father shared the typical Scots urge for education, and the boy read the writings of Bacon and Newton, Swift and Dr. Johnson, which his father had collected.

At the early age of twenty John was appointed works manager in a Dundee power-mill, but within six months he had resigned, refusing to sanction the conditions under which mere children were expected to work long hours for a miserable pittance. He seems to have set up in business on his own account with considerable success, until he was challenged by the claims of the Christian ministry. Under the influence of the Haldane brothers, the founders of Independency in Scotland, he was persuaded to undergo training for the Congregational ministry at the Hoxton Theological Academy in London. Here he went in 1799, learning the theory during the week-days and the practice during the week-ends. He would have been found on any Sunday during the next three years preaching or teaching the under-privileged in London workhouses and slums. Here, as in the Dundee

factory, Philip showed his care for the underdog: this
was to be the rich red thread of compassion with which
the tapestry of his life was to be woven.

His course completed in 1802, he was in the fortunate
position of being able to select a church from among three
cordial invitations issued to him. He chose Newbury
Congregational Church in Berkshire, where he immediately
showed his mettle by advertising a course of Sunday
evening lectures for the benefit of the bucolic community.
Difficulty, it seems, was merely the grindstone on which
Philip sharpened the steel of his intellect. It appears
that his strong Scots accent was an impediment to understanding him. An Anglican curate, recently down from
Oxford, referring to Philip's most recent lecture,
remarked, ' I liked as much of it as I could understand '.
Immediately the minister set himself the task of curbing
the barbaric asperities of his accent, apparently with
success!

In 1804 he became minister of the most influential
Congregational Church in Aberdeen, where he remained
for fourteen years. While here, he was appointed as the
resident Director of the London Missionary Society, which
had been founded only nine years before his arrival, and
had sent out Dr. van der Kemp to be its Director of
Missions in South Africa the year before Philip entered
theological College. It is one of the remarkable coinci-
dences of history that one of Philip's church members
should have been George Thom. This man was later to
become the Superintendent of L.M.S. missions in South
Africa, and later still a minister of the Dutch Reformed
Church in the Cape. It was the Rev. Dr. George Thom
who, in 1822, returned from Scotland to the Cape Colony
with the Rev. Andrew Murray senior, and thus immeasurably enriched the ministry of the Dutch Reformed
Church with a veritable tribe of Murrays who were men
of God.

Philip's advocacy of the cause of missions was to bring him to the notice both of North America and of London. In 1819 he was awarded the honorary Doctorate of Divinity both of Columbia and Princeton Universities. About the same time his fellow Directors of the London Missionary Society showed their esteem by inviting Philip to become a member of the Society's deputation to South Africa, to set the affairs of its missions on an even keel, and possibly to remain there as Superintendent of Missions.

Thus it was that Dr. Philip came to land at Cape Town on 26 February in 1819, accompanied by Dr. Campbell and by Mrs. Philip. Philip married Jane Ross, the daughter of an outstanding bridge-designer and engineer, in 1809. She proved to be an invaluable companion, hostess and colleague for thirty-eight years. She controlled all the finances of the L.M.S. in South Africa, and carefully superintended her husband's personal expenditure. John Philip may have lived for fourteen years in Aberdeen, but he would have emptied his purse into the hands of the first vagrant who appealed for his help. Jane was, therefore, a guard on John's excessive generosity. Practical and efficient as she was, she was yet most human. This gem, extracted from her love letters to a husband frequently away from home on business, reveals her humanity: ' Pray remember ', she wrote in 1836, ' I am still flesh and not all spirit.'

Fortified by such a wife, Philip undertook the gigantic task of reorganizing the London missions in South Africa. He remained at his post for thirty gruelling years, until at the age of seventy he was worn out in the Society's service. At least as often as every second year he went on long ox-wagon treks to visit the mission stations, some of which were as remote from his Cape Town headquarters as Kuruman and Taungs or Kaffraria. His energy and courage are evidenced in his visit, at the age of sixty-seven, to the astute Chief Moshesh in distant

Thaba Bosiu in 1842. During these years his stations totalled over thirty, and he was directly responsible for financing, staffing and planning the policy of each one of them. At the same time he was the minister of the Union Congregational Church in Cape Town, which was built in 1822.

The reader may well ask: surely such a task was so engrossing that Philip should not have had time to meddle with politics? The answer Philip himself made to this reiterated criticism is instructive. He said of his opponents: 'Nothing is *politics* for them but the advocacy of the rights of the oppressed.' The fact was that Philip believed that the repressive race-attitudes of both the government and the Colonists were interfering with the success of his missionary institutions. For their part, they believed that his liberalism was making the Christian Hottentots unwilling to remain in a state of servitude. The Coloured man or the Native naturally looked to the missionary to mediate between themselves and the powerful White society of which the missionary was a member. Professor Macmillan says: 'Of necessity, the modern missionary must be a politician.' We may agree wholeheartedly, provided he does not become a partisan and a party-politician!

At first Dr. Philip was not an opponent, but an admired leader of the Colonists. It is significant that in 1824 he was asked to become chairman of the Distressed Settlers' Fund, and in that capacity assisted in the rehabilitation of the Settlers of the Eastern Province who had suffered grievously from a catastrophic flood following upon a searing drought. His unpopularity began when he championed the cause of the Hottentots against their oppressors, as he believed the Colonists to be.

The greater his achievements in removing causes of oppression, the greater grew his unpopularity among the alleged oppressors. His achievements were, in fact, considerable. He was in close contact with Wilberforce, Buxton and Dr. Lushington in England, the ' triumvirate ' of the Clapham Sect, pledged to abolish slavery throughout the British Empire. Through them he urged that a Government Commission of Inquiry should be set up to investigate the wrongs of the Coloured people in the Cape. When the Commissioners visited the Cape in 1823, no man was more assiduous than Philip in collecting evidence of oppression.

His next concern was to make the administration of justice in the Colony more prompt and efficient. He was in correspondence with Sir Richard Ottley, one of His Majesty's Judges in Ceylon, and on his advice drew up a memorandum on the Cape Courts of Justice. The reforms, when they came, were modelled very much on the lines of Philip's plan.

The power of Philip's overseas influence and his inflexible courage were next seen in the campaign he waged against the autocracy of the Governor, Lord Charles Somerset. Somerset proceeded to suppress the radical newspaper, the *Commercial Advertiser,* which was run by Philip's friends, Pringle and Fairbairn, because they presumed to offer constructive criticisms of his administration. It was Philip who took up the cudgels on behalf of a free press. It was also, in part, Philip's correspondence with Buxton that helped to remove Somerset from office. In the same way Philip influenced the decision of the Secretary to recall Sir Benjamin D'Urban in 1837.

Perhaps his greatest influence was realized in the promulgation of the famous Ordinance No. 50 ' for improving the condition of the Hottentots and other free persons of Colour . . .' which was issued in 1828. At this time Philip was in London recording the abuses under which the Non-European in the Colony smarted. The new Ordinance either removed or mitigated such disadvantages as: the legal disability to hold land, the pass system, summary imprisonment, and forced labour and apprenticeship. It is certain that when this Ordinance was first drafted, Philip was consulted, and that he urged that any possibility of early repeal of it by a Governor of the Cape Colony should be prevented by a final clause, requiring the express approval of His Majesty's Government for any modification. This act, hardly as it may have borne on farmers and employers of labour, was none the less the highwater-mark of Cape liberal legislation, and no single man had contributed as much to secure its adoption as Philip.

During his London stay, he published his *Researches in South Africa* (its sub-title might well have been ' Strictures on South Africa '), and its catalogue of indictments roused the Colonists to fury. Philip returned to the Cape to find that Mackay (named in the *Researches*), the Deputy Landdrost of Somerset East, had brought a libel action against him, denying Philip's charge that he had abused his authority in oppressing the Hottentots. To the undisguised pleasure of the Colonists, Philip lost the action, judgment being given for the plaintiff for £200 damages and £900 costs. These heavy charges were met by Philip's friends in England.

Limits of space forbid a detailed account of Philip's later career. Suffice it to state that he made two suggestions of far-reaching political importance. In the first place, he advocated positive *apartheid* (or, to use the contemporary term ' vertical segregation ') in the interests of the Non-Europeans. In his missionary industrial institutions he anticipated the provision of protected labour ' reserves ', believing that this offered his charges the best protection from commercial and agricultural exploitation. It was his distinction to realize so long ago that the Non-Europeans must be integrated into the national economy, not only in the capacity of well-trained producers, but also as consumers. His theories were proved by the fact

that the L.M.S. institution at Zuurbrak was able to supply
two shops exclusively with the products of the mission.
Philip was also one of the first to experiment with the
growing of hemp and cotton seed at his institutions. He
was no friend of assimilation or miscegenation, but his
segregation policy was conceived in the interests of
Eurafricans and Africans.

His second proposal of importance was made during
the Kaffir Wars, when he advocated the creation of a belt
of Native states to the north and east of the Cape Colony,
as the guarantors of frontier peace. It seemed for a time
as if treaties might be made on these lines, but the
futility of the plan was shown on the outbreak of the
Kaffir War of 1846. Philip's disappointment was the
keener because his son-in-law, Fairbairn, now withdrew
his moral support, and his convert Jan Tschatshuo (whom
he had taken ' on tour ' in England) treacherously joined
the invading Kaffir bands.

The rest of Philip's days were lived in political
quietude, but also, alas, in domestic tragedy. His eldest
son, William, a most promising missionary, was accident-
ally drowned in the Gamtoos River near Hankey Mission
Station, in 1845. Two years later the second blow fell,
in the death of his beloved wife and companion, Jane.
In 1849 he resigned his post at Cape Town, returning to
the solitude of his favourite mission station at Hankey,
where he died in 1851.

What were the achievements of his long and militant
life? He became the first and the most vigorous champion
of the under-privileged Coloured peoples of South Africa.
By his unruffled courage he had ' put down the mighty
from their seats ' and he had assisted in removing two
Governors from their pedestals. Men called him a political parson, a visionary prophet. In fact, however, his
knowledge of conditions in and beyond the Cape Colony
was unrivalled, as was his determination to collect the

data of oppression. His magnetic and compassionate mind had drawn to him a wide circle of influential friends and crusaders against oppression. His letters reveal that 'the most unpopular man in South Africa' was esteemed by a group which included Sir John Herschel, the astronomer, General Sir James Alexander, Sir Jahleel Brenton of the Admiralty, the Principals of King's and Marischal Colleges in the University of Aberdeen, Sir Richard Ottley, Sir Thomas Fowell Buxton, and members of the British Cabinet.

This 'meddling politician' was also chief adviser to the French missions in Basutoland and to the American missions in Natal and Zululand. In fact, on his advice the parent societies, sponsoring these missions, selected their respective fields of operation.

The cynic might be disposed to ask: What benefits did Philip receive from his championship of the Coloured? The answer is: Increasing animosity from members of his own race. His estate on his death was valued at £2,300 and it will be remembered that he married the daughter of a substantial Scottish business man.

He had his faults, it is true. Among them were a disposition to believe that every story of oppression was true, and every exculpation a mere rationalization; and he was a trifle pompous. The ship in which he travelled to England in 1826 almost collided with another vessel, which seemed to run under her stern. Philip's comment on his deliverance was: 'My first feelings were gratitude to God that the cause of the Coloured population of South Africa was not buried with me in the deep.' In his lonely struggle perhaps he did not overstate his role in the drama of emancipation.

Despite Prof. Macmillan's splendidly just account of Philip, the Union is not yet ready to recognize him as one of its heroes. But such courage, integrity and political grasp of affairs, welded to the cause of the oppressed, will make Philip's stature grow with the years. For he, more than any man, saw the Eurafrican and the African, not as problems, nor as conveniences, but as men and potential citizens of the earthly kingdom, and actual citizens of the Kingdom of God. He can afford to wait for a delayed recognition, for he is with the immortals.

CHAPTER III

ROBERT MOFFAT OF KURUMAN

EVERY missionary is a man-tamer, but of whom else except Moffat can it be said that he tamed two of the most feared men in Southern Africa? One of them was Africaner, a Hottentot commander who carried a price of 1,000 rix-dollars on his head; the other was Mzilikazi, the horrific chief of the Matebele. As the man who first reduced Sechuana (the language of the Bechuana) to writing and then translated the whole of the Bible into this tongue, he is commemorated in the Bible House of London in a stained-glass window, where he companies with Jerome and Tyndale, Martin Luther and Robert Morrison, among other great translators. London honoured Moffat's fifty-three years of service in South African missions by according him its highest distinction: the Freedom of the City. Edinburgh, the Athens of the North, awarded him the Honorary Doctorate of Divinity of its University. Whether as evangelist, educationalist, agriculturalist, explorer or writer, he is pre-eminent in all spheres, and only excelled in some by his famous son-in-law, David Livingstone.

Yet it was the man that impressed his contemporaries, even more than his dazzling achievements. An acquaintance gives us a most vivid verbal portrait of him in his closing years: ' The shaggy grey beard adorned the face sunburnt by the exposure of half a century to the heat of Africa; while his piercing black eyes betokened the spirit of one who had often stood face to face with all that was most fierce, whether wild beast or savage, or twinkled with the keenest humour and heartiest humanity.' Obituary notices usually flatter, but this one drew Moffat

to the life in all his courage and integrity, and both
virtues were really the fruits of a deep trust in the power
of the risen Christ, Who walked with Moffat down the
South African roads.

Like so many South African missionaries of distinction,
he was a Scotsman. Ormiston, Fife, was his birthplace,
and, significantly, he was born in the same year as the
London Missionary Society, in 1795. When Robert was
three, his father obtained some obscure post in the Portsoy
customs-house. Nine years later the entire Moffat family
moved to Carronshore, on the northern bank of the Firth
of Forth, where the lad voyaged far in his imagination,
as he was later to do in reality. His education was brief,
limited and seriously interrupted. It comprised little more
than an ability to read the *Shorter Catechism*, when he
ran away to sea. At the age of eleven, however, the
hardened sailor retired from this disenchanting career,
and studied for six months in a Falkirk school, where he
learned book-keeping and writing. Geography and
astronomy, it seems, were extras for the sons of the
wealthy — these Moffat learned by eavesdropping, the
only way possible for him. One suspects that the real
dominie of the seven Moffat children was their mother,
who made the entire brood (not without masculine pro-
test) sew and knit during the long winter evenings
while she read them exciting episodes from the narratives
of the Moravian missionaries in Greenland or the East
Indies. It is amazing to reflect that at this very time,
Mary Smith (the future Mrs. Robert Moffat) was probably hearing the same sagas of the Gospel in the Moravian
School at Fairfield, Lancashire. In both cases their
imaginations were fired with admiration.

On reaching fourteen Robert was apprenticed to a
gardener at Polmont, who was a just but still a hard man
and who expected his apprentices to be afoot at 4.0 a.m.
in the bitter winter darkness. More than once Robert

had to hammer his knuckles against the sides of his spade to bring some feeling into them! After a long day's work, the lad went to evening-classes to learn Latin and mensuration, a curious combination of culture and technics. A neighbour taught him the blacksmith's art, and the merry consolations of the fiddle. These smatterings of knowledge were to prove most useful, for the demands made upon the versatility of a pioneer missionary are legion. In 1812, he accepted a post on the estate of the Earl of Moray, near Aberdour.

Next he was promoted under-gardener of Mr. Leigh of High Leigh, Cheshire. It was to bring him within the orbit of the influence of the city of Manchester which prided itself, not without cause, for thinking to-day what London thought to-morrow. In this area he found his soul, his vocation and his fiancée. The Wesleyan Methodists helped him to find his soul in the warmth and simplicity of their Society in High Leigh, where the Presbyterian training of his youth and the influence of his devout mother were rekindled. His canny father cautiously advised him to ' follow the sects so far only as they follow the Word of God '. Truths that hitherto had been on the top of his mind were transferred to the bottom of his heart. In brief, he was converted.

His vocation was discovered almost by accident, if it is right to assume that there are any accidents in a Divinely-controlled universe. He was going into Warrington to make a small purchase, when his eye was held by a poster, announcing that the Rev. William Robey was to take the chair at a missionary rally. To his chagrin, he noticed that it was already out of date. No matter, for his imagination was seized by the possibility of missionary work. He determined to call on Mr. Robey in Manchester. This gentleman immediately saw his zeal and integrity and urged the London Missionary Society to accept Moffat as a candidate. At first the Directors of the Society

refused consent, but yielded when Robey promised to get
Moffat a part-time post near him, and to be responsible
for giving him some theológical instruction.

Thus it was that Moffat came to work for Mr. Smith
of Dukinfield and learned to love the charming, intelli-
gent and devout Miss Mary Smith.   For five days work
he received thirteen shillings a week in wages, the rest
of the time being spent in studying for his vocation. This
part-time training for a few months was all the preparation he had as a missionary.   It seems, now, to have been
designed (if designed at all) to make or break missionaries.   Those who had inner resources of strength and
adaptability became pioneers in the great nineteenth-
century expansion of Christianity.   Those who failed
became a severe embarrassment to their Societies.   Moffat
succeeded beyond the dreams of his sponsors.

In 1816 he bade his parents farewell and did not set
eyes upon them again for twenty-three years.   He was
set apart for his Divine vocation at a great missionary
gathering in London.   Another ordinand was young John
Williams, soon to be the martyr of Erromanga in Poly-
nesia.   He might well have shared the other's end, had
not a Scots Director, Dr. Waugh, objected to sending
them as yoke-fellows, considering ' thae twa lads ower
young to gang together '.   On 18 October 1816, they
sailed for Cape Town on the *Alacrity*, which belied its
name in taking eighty-six days over the journey.

The L.M.S. intended that twenty-one-year-old Moffat
and his companion Kitchingman should proceed to Africaner's Kraal in Namaqualand, then beyond the frontiers
of the Colony, but the Governor refused the necessary
permit.   The Rev. Mr. George Thom, then Superintendent
of the London Missionary Society, used his influence
with the Governor and caused the decision to be reversed.
The intervening months were spent by Moffat at Stellenbosch as the guest of Mynheer Hamman, a wealthy wine-

farmer, in whose home he learned to speak Dutch with fluency. This was to prove an inestimable advantage to him later. In September of 1817 he, Kitchingman and Ebner set off for Africaner's Kraal, to evangelize the collection of vagrant Hottentots under the charge of their brigand chief. On the way north the young man had an opportunity of showing both his convictions and his tact, and of appreciating a courage equal to his own. He had stopped for the night at the farm of a wealthy Dutch patriarch. When supper was over, the host convened the family prayers and invited the missionary to conduct them. 'But where are the servants?' asked Moffat. 'Servants! What do you mean?' countered the patriarch. 'I mean the Hottentots,' said Moffat, 'of whom I see so many on your farm.' Anger mounting, his host retorted, 'Hottentots! Do you mean that, then? Let me go to the mountains and call the baboons, if you want a congregation of that sort. Or stop, I have it: my sons, call the dogs that lie in front of the door. They will do.' The missionary dropped an attempt that would then have led to a violent ending. The psalm sung and the prayer offered, Moffat read the lesson of the Syrophoenician women who asked Jesus to cure her daughter and chose as his text the words, 'Yea, Lord, but even the dogs eat of the crumbs that fall from the master's table.' His host interrupted quietly this time: 'Will *Mynheer* sit down and wait a little? He shall have the Hottentots.' The motley throng trooped in, many of whom had never heard a preacher before nor seen the inside of their master's house. When the service was over, the farmer turned to his guest and said, 'My friend, you took a hard hammer and your have broken a hard head.' One hardly knows which of the two to admire most: Moffat or his host; the tact and courage of the former, or the willingness of the latter to root out publicly a deep prejudice. If courage is needed to declare

God's Word, perhaps even greater courage is required to accept it.

Moffat stayed at Africaner's Kraal for a year. His home in Vredenburg was a willow-cage covered with rush mats, with a ' crawl-hole ' for adit. During this time he did not see another white man, and his only food was milk and biltong. His captivating personality won the trust and the admiration of Africaner, and he was able to lead the chief back to Cape Town as a reformed character. Moffat's friends could not at first believe that he was alive, thinking him a grim denizen of the next world, despatched there by Africaner. A tamed Africaner was a trophy of the triumphant Gospel. The ' trophy ' was introduced to the Governor and the stock of the missionaries was high for some time afterwards.

Moffat's thoughts were often in Manchester, but Mary Smith's parents doted on her and seemed to consider Moffat unworthy of her. Robert wrote rather pointedly, 'A missionary in this country without a wife is like a boat with one oar.' Mary prevailed in time over her parents and came across to marry and to join Moffat in the work late in 1819. A missionary enthusiast of the Congregational Church in Ashton-under-Lyne, she was in fortitude the equal of her husband, for she had a most vivid imagination and much loneliness in which to exercise it, while her husband was away on pioneering work. After their marriage in St. George's Church in Cape Town (to-day the Cathedral Church), they set out for New Lattakoo* among the Bechuana at the beginning of 1820, travelling via Griquatown. In a letter home she comments on the strangeness of the domestic arrangements in Griquatown, noting the provision of detached kitchens, the washing of clothes in cold water and the use of stones as a ' rubbing-board ', and the making of tallow and soap from the fat tails of the sheep. She is enthusiastic about the value of

* Kuruman Mission Station was not founded until 1825.

cow-dung as a flooring material, remarking that 'it lays the dust better than anything, kills the fleas that would otherwise breed abundantly, and is a fine clear green'.

In April 1821 their first daughter, Mary, was born in Kuruman, a name for ever associated with the Moffats. Here the former gardener had made the desert bloom like the rose. He led the water from the great springs in a conduit three miles long, five feet wide and two feet deep, to the mission station; planted the banks with willows and poplars; and fed the large gardens in front of the solid stone mission houses. For years Kuruman was a show-place of Southern Africa and the last outpost of civilization for all missionaries, traders, hunters and explorers who found their genial host a map and signpost to the interior.

Characteristic of Moffat's love for humanity was his adoption of two Bushmen orphans in 1822, when he came unexpectedly upon a party of them digging a grave for a woman. They were proposing to bury the orphans with her, that they might be cared for by their mother in the shades of the other world. Moffat begged to adopt them and, rejoicing in the names of Dicky and Ann, they became an integral part of his own family for years.

At first the work at Kuruman was most disappointing spiritually. Their charges seemed to be shameless thieves and utterly unresponsive to their teaching. In fact this obduracy was only broken by a revival which came after thirteen years of patient preparation. Meanwhile, Moffat was learning Sechuana and translating some hymns and portions of the Scriptures into that language, and erecting the vast Kuruman church which could seat 500. Incidentally, its high roof was a triumph of manual dexterity and strength, for it was raised on the four naked walls without any hoisting tackle. For the timber Moffat had to make a second visit to the country of the Matebele, venturing through 700 miles of virgin territory.

The first of his historic visits to the notorious and bloodthirsty Mzilikazi, the chief of the Matebele, was made at the end of 1829. The chief had sent two emissaries to Kuruman, having heard of the remarkable agricultural and architectural skill of the missionaries. Moffat treated the *indunas* well, but knew that their return to the chief through hostile tribes would mean inevitable death, unless he were to accompany them. He went with them as far as the high veld to the east of what is now Pretoria. In ten days the party reached Mosega (now Zendelings-post, west of Zeerust). The *indunas* now informed him that they dared not return to their chief without Moffat, since he had come so far with them. He therefore con-sented to go further. As they travelled towards the Limpopo, he observed that the Magaliesburg mountains were pock-marked with the ruins of once flourishing villages that had been ransacked and burned by the marauding Matebele or the Mantatis.* In five days they reached the outposts of the Matebele, and on they went through fertile lands that were teeming with rhinoceros and giraffe, and marred only by vast mounds of bleaching bones. (Stow computes that at least a million human beings were sacrificed in the Matebele wars.)

At last they reached their destination, and Moffat the unafraid was probably the first white man to see the dreaded Mzilikazi face to face. They entered a large cattle-fold ' where were ranged in a semi-circle about 800 warriors in full dress. About 300 more sat concealed in ambush, perhaps for precaution or to try our courage.' Moffat stayed there for eight days, and the admiring chieftain laid his hand upon his friend, saying, ' My heart is all white as milk '. Moffat informed him that he had come neither to hunt nor to trade, but as a teacher from God, the Creator, and Christ the Prince of Peace. Even

---

* The Mantatis are the Batlokwa.

then Moffat envisaged the possibility of missionaries being established among the Matebele.

This particular hope was not to be fulfilled until 1857, during the fourth visit to Mzilikazi's Great Place.* This time Livingstone had persuaded the L.M.S to make a two-pronged missionary attack on the Makololo (north of the Zambezi) and the hostile Matebele (south of the Zambezi). Moffat's Matebele reconnoitre was successful and he saw his son John S. Moffat and Messrs. Sykes and Thomas safely settled at Inyati. But the Makololo expedition cost the lives of Mr. and Mrs. Helmore, two of their four children, Mrs. Price and her child, and several of the Bechuana attendants. The full story of this remarkable pioneering work can be read in Robert Moffat's *Matebele Journal*.

To retrace our footsteps, the Moffats took their only furlough in 1840, twenty-three years after he had first set foot on African soil. It is interesting that the famous Baxter print taken at this time shows the normally bearded Moffat clean-shaven. Apparently he was told on the way from Kuruman to Cape Town that beards were unfashionable, so he retired behind a bush and returned looking younger than his forty-three years. Later, of course, he re-grew the familiar long beard. He returned to England to see the Sechuana New Testatment through the press and that he and his wife might recover their health. At first this modest man was taken, because of his noble height and sunburn, for a sea-captain; but once his identity was known he was lionized. So great a throng gathered to hear him in the vast Exeter Hall in London that he had to give his speech twice to two different audiences. Thrilled by Moffat's narrative, David Livingstone was deflected to Africa from his original intention of going to China. To Moffat's great joy Livingstone

---

* By the time of Moffat's fourth visit Mzilikazi had moved his Great Place to the neighbourhood of the present Bulawayo.

and the Rev. William Ross sailed to South Africa as recruits for the L.M.S. field, and brought with them the first 500 copies of the Sechuana New Testament. The claims on Moffat's time as a public speaker made inroads on his health. He secluded himself and wrote his famous *Missionary Labours and Scenes in Southern Africa* in 1841, which was published the following year. Friends in Edinburgh said farewell and presented him with a copy of the *Encyclopedia Britannica* (perhaps Bechuanaland's first library?) and Newcastle friends gave him a set of scientific instruments. The first testified to his insatiable love of knowledge and the second to his acute geological, botanical and meteorological observations.

On his return to the scenes of his labours (1843), David Livingstone came to the Vaal River to meet him. Soon afterwards the young explorer had his famous fight with a lion, and it was while convalescing that he proposed to Mary Moffat under the Kuruman almond-tree. Not long afterwards Moffat also mangled his arm, but in less dramatic circumstances. While setting up a new corn-mill, he unwarily caught his sleeve in the cogs and was only able to stop the machine when it had torn a six-inch gash in his arm. The rest of his long service at Kuruman was spent in translating the Old Testament, in journeys to out-stations, in services and conferences, in prospecting trips, and in consolidating the work.

In the eighteen-sixties he and Mary Moffat had to face a series of family tragedies. His son, Robert, died in 1862; a few months later they heard of Mary Livingstone's death on the Zambezi. In 1866 the husband of another Moffat daughter, the French missionary Frédoux, was literally detonated to death by a nefarious trader. Only the previous year a Bechuana of unsound mind had set upon Moffat with a knobkerrie and nearly battered him to death. It seemed as if the cup of sorrow was being drained to the very dregs. But the grand old man of missions was heartened by the success of the Matebele mission and by the affection in which both the Bechuana and the British held him.

In 1870 he preached his moving farewell sermon to Kuruman. He and Mary Moffat returned to England, but with great reluctance; it seemed that the tragedies recently witnessed made it impossible for them to remain amid the scenes in which they had laboured sacrificially for over fifty years. Soon after their return, the brave spirit of Mary Moffat left her fragile body. Thereafter for some years Moffat led a restless, itinerating life as a public speaker for missions throughout Britain. Then, in 1873, he settled down in Brixton for the last ten years of his long life.

The appreciation of a grateful Britain knew no bounds. Twice he was summoned to meet the Queen; twice he breakfasted with Mr. Gladstone. He received the Freedom of the City of London. He was presented with a gift of £5,000 by his well-wishers which enabled him to contribute handsomely to the needs of his two widowed daughters and their children and left him an old age of moderate comfort. He was invited to lecture in Westminster Abbey, where the bones of his distinguished son-in-law were interred, and Dr. Casalis arranged for him to be fêted in Paris by the Evangelical Missionary Society there. He died in 1883, crowned with honour. The London *Times* leader which saluted his memory found an echo of appreciation throughout South Africa and Britain. It concluded: ' Robert Moffat has died in the fullness both of years and of honours. His work has been to lay the foundations of the Church in the central regions of South Africa. His name will be remembered while the South African Church endures, and his example will remain with us as a stimulus to others and as an abiding proof of what a Christian missionary can be and do.'

CHAPTER IV

WILLIAM SHAW

WILLIAM SHAW was one of the greatest of the Union's adopted sons and his claim to fame rests upon three foundations. He was the only minister of religion who accompanied the 1820 British Settlers to Algoa Bay and shared their hopes and anxieties in the first years in Albany. He was a missionary strategist and planner of the highest order: at the time of his retirement his one station had become fifty-one stations. Hardly had he entered the Eastern Province when he was planning a chain of mission stations to link Algoa and Delagoa Bays. He left one of the most fascinating historical and travelling narratives ever published, entitled, *The Story of My Mission to South-East Africa*. He is commemorated on the map of his adopted country by the mission station named Shawbury and in the magnificent missionary achievements of the Methodist Church of South Africa, which has more African members than any other Church in the Union.

Little is known of his life before 1820, and so that part of the story can soon be told. His father was a respected member of the North York Militia, which was stationed in Glasgow at the time of his birth in 1798. He was the eleventh child of the family, the parents being devout Anglicans. Their intention that he should take a commission was frustrated by his conversion and connection with the Wesleyan Society in Harwich in 1812. He moved with his father's regiment to Ireland and to East Anglia. Meantime, he was a local preacher. In 1816 he set up his own school at Long Sutton and in the

30

same year (at the age of eighteen) married Miss Ann Maw. His marriage seemed to preclude any possibility of his entering the home ministry, but made his application to accompany the 1820 Settlers more acceptable, so it appears.

This event was brought about by the speech of Vansittart, Chancellor of the British Exchequer, who urged the House of Commons to stem the rising tide of unemployment after the Napoleonic wars by an immigration scheme, to be subsidized by a parliamentary grant of £50,000. The second purpose of this mass emigration was to put a stop to further Native depredations of the Cape Colony by using the Settlers as a buffer. This, however, was not stated in the speech which painted the Eastern Province in the colours of Paradise. The Chancellor said: 'The Cape is suited to the productions both of temperate and warm climates, to the olive, the mulberry, and the vine, as well as to most culmiferous and leguminous plants: *and the persons emigrating to this settlement would soon find themselves comfortable.*' Faced with stern reality, the Settlers did not readily forgive the Chancellor this flight of fancy! Out of a total of 90,000 applicants, 4,000 selected emigrants were permitted to leave England. The Government was prepared to meet the cost of a minister's salary (£100 per annum) for any party of not less than a hundred families which was willing to share the services of a minister. Thus it was that Shaw came over to South Africa as the chaplain of a number of Wesleyan families and their friends.

William Shaw accepted the appointment as minister among the Colonists largely because it offered a springboard for missionary work. It is clear that only a man of intrepid will and unclouded faith could have maintained his enthusiasm during the general disillusionment of the early years. From the moment of their arrival in Algoa Bay the Settlers discovered that the Eastern Frontier was not the land flowing with milk and honey of which they had dreamed. The future Port Elizabeth had not even the semblance of a harbour in 1820 and the city of the future consisted of one house and a small military outpost named Fort Frederick. Shaw's party was not impressed as they travelled on loaned ox-wagons through the thick bush up the Assegai River valley. Their guide, Colonel Cuyler, bade then a sinister farewell: ' Gentlemen, when you go out to plough never leave your guns behind.' The Settlers lived first in tents and then in improvised dwellings of wattle-and-daub. Shaw's first home was a single room twelve feet square, contructed of twigs and mud. He and his plucky wife slept amid the rafters under the unlined thatch and probably dreamed of the ample four-poster they had left behind in East Anglia.

The Cockney wit and adaptability of the Sephton* party stood them in good stead in the first months. One man whose ground consisted of little else but stones, and who wished to change it for more promising land, found the authorities in Grahamstown stone-deaf to his complaints. Remembering that the Government had reserved a right to any minerals or jewels found on the allocated lands, the man informed the unheeding official that he had many precious stones. The hitherto deaf official pricked up his ears, and thundered, ' What kind of precious stones?' Quick came the rejoinder, 'Precious *big* stones!' The Settlers had a genius for producing substitutes for unobtainable luxuries: the leaves of a Cape shrub made tea; roasted barley did duty for coffee-beans, and dried potato-tops provided ersatz-tobacco! Despite this, they were so healthy that the doctors who accompanied them sought other posts because they were unemployed among the Settlers.

* The name of the party of Settlers to which Shaw was attached.

In the first three or four years the emigrants had to
face disaster after disaster. The first wheat crop was
destroyed by rust. The next year a searing sun and
drought burned up the harvest. This, in turn, was succeeded by a torrential flood which carried crops, cattle
and even houses on its swollen waters. William Shaw,
their natural leader, must have required inner resources of
faith to keep cheerful in these days.

It was decided to name their new home 'Salem', in
the hope that they would remain undisturbed by Native
invaders. A deserted farm-house was requisitioned, under
Shaw's orders, as a community centre. The main room,
some sixty feet long and twelve broad, served as town
hall, stores, lying-in hospital and church. To adapt this
derelict building for the purpose of Divine worship
required imagination, and this Shaw had in abundance.
He wrote: 'For lack of a pulpit, I was accustomed to stand
on a small box; and a writing-desk, placed on top of an
American flour-barrel, behind which I stood, formed
the resting-place for the Bible and other books used in
public worship.' They had no pews; each family brought
its own chairs and benches to each service. On one
occasion, when Shaw was addressing a class meeting, a
member jumped up, crying, 'Sir, there is a puff-adder
beneath your feet!'

The untamed bush was full of hazards, especially for a
conscientious minister who visited his farming flock on
foot. Often the cries of leopards and wolves broke on
the still evening air. At such cries Shaw used to imitate
Zacchaeus, shinning up the nearest tree and remaining
there until the light of day released him from his cramped
posture. On his later missionary travels he remained un-
moved by the sight of hippopotami at close range in the
rivers, or herds of elephant in the bush. Indeed, he was
once rebuked by his faithful servant, Kotongo, for adven-
turing in the bush without a gun. When the missionary

replied that the Natives knew him as a *Fundis*,* Kotongo retorted, 'But I doubt whether the elephants will recognize you as a *Fundis*!'

Shaw determined to build up the work amongst the Europeans first, believing that this would constitute a base from which to launch pioneering missionary work. To that end services were commenced at Grahamstown, a growing town, which had developed by the middle of the last century into the second largest city in the Cape Colony. Shaw's keenest helpers were Sergeants Lucas and Price, stationed in Grahamstown. Methodism, it may be remarked in passing, owes much to British soldiers for they established Methodism in Cape Town and in the British Colonies of North America. The Methodist system of training local preachers as ministerial auxiliaries has reaped handsome spiritual dividends. In Grahamstown, Shaw proved himself a man of faith for, when the foundation stone of the first Methodist Church in Chapel Street was laid in 1821, he required about £500 and he had only half a crown in hand! Shaw once said, ' I belong to a sect but I am no sectarian at heart.' This he proved by lending his chapel to the Anglicans before St. George's Church (later the Cathedral) was built. It was the same appreciation of the Anglican heritage in worship that caused him to be elected Convenor of a Committee of British Conference in 1872 to draw up a Methodist *Book of Offices* on the model of the *Book of Common Prayer*.

As the work among Europeans in the Albany district was being consolidated, William Shaw felt able to embark on missionary development. Other missionary societies insisted that their representatives should devote themselves only to missionary work, and, as a consequence, they were often able to report spectacular, if not long-lived, results.

---

* *Fundis* is, of course, an abbreviation of *umfundisi*, meaning ' minister '.

Time has, however, vindicated the policy of the Methodists which enabled their missionary work to become self-supporting, largely because the man who ministered to the Colonists was also the pastor of the Africans. Moreover, many of the European local preachers were found to have the makings of excellent missionaries. The Rev. William Shepstone, for many years Shaw's right-hand man, is one case in point.

Shaw's apostolical plan for a chain of mission stations along the coast from the Eastern Province to Natal was formulated only a few months after arriving in the Cape Colony. He wrote these prophetic words in his report to the Mission House in London:

> I hope the Committee will never forget that with the exception of Lattakoo, which is far in the interior, there is not a single missionary station between the place of my residence and the northern extremity of the Red Sea. . . . Here then is a wide field — the whole Eastern coast of the continent of Africa. If ever the words of the Saviour were applicable to any part of the world at any time, surely they apply to Eastern Africa at the present time: *The harvest is great, but the labourers are few.*

Considering the smallness of his resources in money and man-power, he pushed forward his plans with amazing rapidity. In 1823 the first of his stations was founded among the subjects of chief Pato and named Wesleyville. Two years later Mount Coke was established in memory of Dr. Thomas Coke the famous early Methodist missionary: it was designed to serve the subjects of chief Dhlami who had been one of the leaders of the Native attack on Grahamstown only six years before! The third link in the chain was forged in 1827 and named Butterworth after a British M.P. of that name who was the Lay General Treasurer of the Wesleyan Methodist Missionary Society. It lay in the heart of the Pondo country. The fifth link was forged in 1830 and named Clarkebury, after the famous Dr. Adam Clarke, the Biblical commentator of his day. Only a few months later Buntingville was founded to commemorate the famous Secretary of the Methodist Conference, Dr. Jabez Bunting, who has been called ' the second founder of Methodism ', but who is also known to the social historian as having said, ' Methodism agrees as well with democracy as it does with sin.' Two further stations completed the chain. One of them was fittingly named Shawbury, after Shaw himself (though not at his suggestion!), and the eighth was named Palmerton, as a tribute to another distinguished South African Methodist missionary. Thus in a matter of twenty-five years from Shaw's landing in South Africa his dream was realized. One of the most remarkable stations was Butterworth because it ministered to the spiritual needs of the subjects of chief Hintsa, famous for his part in the attack on Grahamstown in 1819. That he should have accepted a British missionary is a tribute to Shaw's daring and to the power of reconciliation in the Christian faith.

The greatness of Shaw's achievement can be statistically assessed. In 1820 he was the only Methodist missionary in South-East Africa; in 1860 there were 36 missionaries and 96 school-teachers and catechists on the field. In 1820 there were 63 church members; in 1860 there were 4,825 full members and 856 members on trial.   In 1820 there were 3 Sunday schools; in 1860 there were 80 Sunday schools and 48 day schools.   In 1820 there were no church buildings; in 1860, 74 chapels had been erected and 183 preaching-stations. The revenue in 1820 was £10 per annum; in 1860 it was £3,500 per annum, exclusive of pew-rents and subscriptions towards the erection of buildings. By 1860 the Word of God was proclaimed by the Methodists in four languages: English, Dutch Xhosa and Sechuana, and by means of two printing presses a few African tribes were able to read parts of the Bible

in the vernacular. For that achievement the greater part
of the credit, under God, must go to William Shaw, who
was as distinguished a missionary and administrator as he
was a minister.

Our account of his work in South Africa cannot conclude without giving two glimpses of his experiences as
a missionary in Kaffraria. The first incident reveals the
misunderstanding to which even the best friends of
the Africans, the missionaries, were subject. One evening
the Natives of a neighbouring clan attacked the Africans
of the Wesleyville district. The missionaries, as befitted
the emissaries of the Prince of Peace, held aloof from the
fray. When it was over they found three enemy corpses
on the battlefield, and a severely wounded man. They
interred the bodies decently, despite the protests of their
charges that these corpses should be left to the tender
mercies of vultures and jackals. They nursed the wounded
man back to life, much to the resentment of his former
enemies, and often the missionaries caught their converts
stealing the sick man's nourishment. One day, however,
Shaw was delighted to hear the Natives explaining his
action in the words, 'The missionaries are the servants
of God and therefore the friends of all.' Then came the
turn of the missionaries to be perplexed. One night the
sick man, almost completely recovered, ran off without a
word of gratitude to Shaw. Later the missionary discovered the reason: the man was afraid that the 'Christian
witch-doctors' would make an exorbitant demand for his
cattle by way of medical fees!

The people among whom he laboured were at that time
untouched by civilization. For example, when the first
plough was introduced to Wesleyville, a young chief
clapped his hands with delight, exclaiming, 'This thing
that the white people have brought is as good as ten
wives!' The religion of the Africans constituted a
challenge to the missionaries, and William Shaw gives a

graphic report of a duel of wills he had with a famous
rain-maker, Gqindiva, whose help had been sought by
chief Pato in time of severe drought. Shaw interrogated
the rain-maker, and urged that rain came from God, not
from the rain-maker. He remarked, rather acidly, on
the curious fact that Gqindiva claimed to control the
rains and yet the crops on his own fields were shrivelled up.
The rain-maker replied that he was hindered from making
rain. Shaw demanded to know who the hindrance was.
The rain-maker answered dramatically, pointing to Shaw,
' *You* are the hindrance!' A serious situation now arose.
Some of Shaw's people believed that his word was stronger
than the rain-maker's; others were obviously sceptical of
the power of the missionary's God. Faced with Elijah's
predicament, he had no alternative but to appeal to God
to vindicate the true prophet, and expose the false. So
he set apart a whole day for fasting and prayer and at
certain intervals called the people together to petition God
for the mercy of rain. The incident is best concluded in
Shaw's own words:

> God was pleased in His infinite mercy to answer for Him-
> self. Just as the people were beginning to assemble for the
> evening service (the last for the day), drops of rain began to
> fall slowly . . . and at the time of its close, the rain was
> falling in heavy showers.

The ' rain-maker ' was discredited and the people called
the downpour of many days ' God's Rain '.

After thirty-seven remarkable years of labour in South
Africa Shaw returned to England, where he ministered in
various Methodist circuits for only eight years, when
English Methodism gave him its finest compliment by
inviting him to be President of the Conference (1865).
Thus England and South Africa paid tribute to a man in
whom dignity and humour, vision and practical sagacity,
were allied. He was pre-eminently a man of faith, rightly

described by his colleagues in England in the following words: 'Among uncommon missionaries William Shaw was one whom His Master had uncommonly honoured.' His faith has been vindicated by the growth of the Methodist Missionary Church in South Africa which in this year of grace numbers no less than 411,416* African souls.

* 1950 figures.

CHAPTER V

DANIEL LINDLEY

HISTORY is full of surprises. Who would have guessed that the first regular minister the Voortrekkers had was an American missionary of English descent? Daniel Lindley, for that was his name, ministered to the trekking Boers for seven happy years, when he held the largest parish any man has ever had in South Africa, for it included the emigrants in Natal, the Free State, and the Transvaal. The rest of his days was spent in labouring amongst the Zulus in Natal, where he established the famous mission station of Inanda and, with Theophilus Shepstone, was responsible for the demarcation of Native Reserves in that Province. He was a missionary, a social anthropologist, a statesman, a pioneer traveller, and a crack shot. More important, he was the friend of God and of men of all races. His name deserves a foremost place on the distinguished roll of the Union's adopted sons. He is commemorated by a town in the Orange Free State, and one of the larger South African planes was named in his honour during the last war. His life should be better known. Now, indeed, that Dr. Edwin Smith has produced his authoritative and fascinating book entitled *The Life and Times of Daniel Lindley, 1801-1880*, there is no reason why this Voortrekker of God's Kingdom should not be widely honoured.

The Lindleys of the United States came of English Puritan stock, and Daniel's father was a respected Presbyterian minister, trained at an institution which has since become world-famous as Princeton University. The first child of Jacob Lindley was born in 1801 at Ten Mile

Creek in Western Pennsylvania. Daniel's upbringing must have been stern, if we are to trust the cadaverous look of Jacob Lindley and the report that he used to hold the feet and arms of his children firmly, when they were only three months old, to break their wills! In such a home the future minister of the Voortrekkers learned self-discipline and endurance. Such time as could be spared from his Spartan studies was spent in the woods of Ohio where panthers, wolves, bear, deer and wild turkeys (weighing forty pounds) abounded. Frontiersmen in those days had to be good shots, and Daniel could bring a squirrel tumbling from the topmost branches with a single shot. On a single day he and his brother shot and hauled home three deer.

He was educated at the local University of Athens, where the curriculum was appropriately and heavily classical in content. His classmates included Negroes of distinction, and his later appreciation of the Zulus owed much to this introduction to the academic African. He was a leading light in the debating society, which must have caused the staff some anxiety, for not only did it boast cuspidors among the furniture, but it chose to debate the topic: ' Is it necessary for a student whose design is to be useful to the community to obtain a critical knowledge of the classics?'

In 1824, now a B.A., he went up to Hampden-Sydney Theological College in Virginia for ministerial training. After only a year there his funds ran out, and with typical independence he refused to be subsidized by a wealthy colonel, preferring to earn his living for three years by teaching. Having saved the necessary expenses, he returned to complete his training in 1831.

He was ordained as minister of the Presbyterian Church of Rocky River, North Carolina, where during his two years' stay 250 persons were added to the roll. An even greater accomplishment was his success in persuading 500

men of Scots and Irish stock to take the temperance pledge
when they had almost unlimited supplies of whisky ('full
of the mule's heels') at sixpence a gallon! These hard-
boiled men liked his fearless preaching and virile outlook.
He might have remained there happily for the rest of
his days had he not heard the call of the foreign mission
field.

At that time the interdenominational American Board
of Commissioners for Foreign Missions was urging ministers to leave settled pastorates to evangelize the non-
Christian world. Soon after Lindley was accepted by the
American Board, he married Lucy Allen of Richmond, a
devoted campaigner against the slave-trade, who was to
be his partner in all enterprises for the next forty-three
years. On 3 December, 1834, they set sail from Boston
and glimpsed the shores of South Africa through the mist
on 5 February, 1835. Champion wrote in his diary: 'It
was Africa we saw — we could not doubt it. Our souls
leaped for joy. Long-wished-for, long-prayed-for Africa,
may we prove a blessing to thy sons and daughters.' Few
prayers have been answered so completely.

The party of American missionaries went to interview
Dr. John Philip at Cape Town, who laughed at their
anxieties about the climate, saying, 'Tell your friends that
missionaries never die here'. Then the party divided: one
section was to remain in Cape Town to learn the Dutch
language and then to go by sea to Natal, as soon as the
Kaffir disturbances concluded; the others (including the
Lindleys) were bound for the far north where Mzilikazi's
people, the Matebele, lived. They prepared to make the
long and almost unknown journey a thousand miles into
the hinterland by ox-wagon. Passing through Worcester
and the Hex River Kloof, they crossed the Little and the
Great Karroo and were appalled at the lack of water.
Thence they crossed the Sneeuberge to the high veld,
fording the Orange River and making their first prolonged

stop at Griqua Town, where their first child Mary was born. They were not idle, however, but learned the Sechuana tongue, finding its complexity and copiousness problems. Lindley remarked that ' the paradign of a Sichuana verb when fully written out is little less in size than a map of the U.S.A.' The next stop was Kuruman, Moffat's station where the women and children were left, whilst Venable and Lindley set out for Mosega, near Kapeng, Mzilikazi's great place '. This they found in the basin between the beginnings of the Molopo and Marico Rivers. They pulled down part of the mission house left by some French missionaries and rebuilt and enlarged it for their three families. Then they sought out the chief who showed them the utmost cordiality. Lindley and a missionary colleague left their wives and children behind at Kuruman whilst they journeyed south for equipment and provisions. Mrs. Lindley wrote: ' Many Natives visited us to-day and expressed much satisfaction that we had come. They regard us females with great curiosity, wondering at our long hair.'

So promising a beginning to the mission ended in two lightning strokes of tragedy: first, the dangerous illness of the missionaries, and then the decimation of their Native neighbours by attack. The fever originated in the damp walls of their newly-built quarters and only the doctor, Wilson, did not fall a prey to this wasting illness. When Mrs. Wilson died, only Lindley was able to crawl off his mattress to assist in her burial rites.

In this disspirited state a second disaster befell them. As it happened, Sarel Cilliers and Hendrik Potgieter* were fairly near neighbours on the banks of the Sand River. They, having been attacked by Mzilikazi's warriors at Vegkop, when they put up a magnificent defence (some forty Boers against a force fifty times as strong), deter-

* Two leaders of the emigrant Boers, who had trekked from the Cape Colony.

mined on a punitive expedition, and early in January 1837 they set out for Mosega. On the 17th Lindley was awakened before sunrise by the cries of terrified Natives, screaming, 'A commando! A commando!' Before the the echoes had died, the Boers opened fire on a kraal a few hundred yards away. The warriors were not in the kraals, but the Boers did not wait to discover that. A terrific slaughter took place before Lindley's eyes, and Mrs. Lindley's rooms were soon filled with bleeding and terrified fugitives. All the neighbouring villages were destroyed and their inhabitants killed or scattered. This was an end of a chapter of Lindley's hopes. He knew that future prospects for missions among the Matebele were doomed for him, and that Mzilikazi would probably forbid him to stay. He therefore decided to throw in his lot with the Boers for the time being, hoping ultimately to reach the maritime party of American missionaries in Natal.

He therefore trekked with the Boers as far as the Vaal River where they encamped. Here, it seems, Lindley's marksmanship impressed his Afrikaner companions mightily. Their crack shot, Naude, invited Lindley to go shooting steenbuck with him on the lee of a neighbouring hill. They agreed to take alternate shots at the buck until one of them should miss. Lindley killed six in six shots, but Naude missed the target with his sixth aim. He congratulated the American with the words: '*Amper so goed soos 'n Afrikaner!*' His standing with these men was high because he proved himself their equal as swimmer, horseman and marksman.

They now parted with the majority of the company, Lindley undertaking in all a 1,300-mile trek from Mosega to Port Natal through Kaffraria. His wife proved as hardy as he. For the last six hundred miles Lucy rode on horseback, using a man's saddle, and 'carrying a child with her, with the expectation of another'. At one point, when they were descending a steep mountain, one of the wagon-wheels was crushed to splinters. They repaired it on the instant ' with an auger, a saw, an axe, and a drawing-knife for instruments, and green wood which we baked in the ground one day, and ourselves as workmen, we repaired the damage very substantially '. Such stout hearts and skilled hands were invincible! Their long journey was completed on 27 July, when they were escorted by Dr. and Mrs. Newton Adams to their new home in Umlazi.

Even here trouble was to dog their footsteps. They had hardly settled in their new home when news came of Dingaan's treacherous massacre of Piet Retief's men. The position of all Europeans in Natal became precarious, and the American Board advised its Natal missionaries to leave the Colony for ever. They were not defeatists, so they merely took a year's working holiday in the Eastern Province. During this time Lindley's thoughts were often with the Boers of Natal, and he was convinced that the opportunities of evangelizing the Zulus would be increased tenfold if a settled minister could further the Christian education of the Trekkers.

After the Battle of Blood River had clipped the talons of Dingaan, life was reasonably secure in Natal. Lindley and his family returned. Meanwhile, the People's Council (' Volksraad ') was set up by the Trekkers on Bushman's Ridge, now renamed Pietermaritzburg, in October of 1838. At the request of the Volksraad, Lindley and his family came to minister to the Boers in 1841. He received a salary of about £100 per annum, with the free use of the *pastorie*. He conducted services in the Church of the Vow, erected in fulfilment of Andries Pretorius's oath before the Battle of Blood River. This Church, built in the centre of Pietermaritzburg, continued to be used for worship until 1861, and in 1912 it was opened as the Voortrekkers' Museum. Lindley's work is best described in his own words: ' I had for my parish all the

country embraced in the district of Natal, the Free State
and the Transvaal Republic. I was sole minister for all
the extended territory I have named, and had the cure
of, I suppose, not less than twenty thousand souls.' So
familiar did he become with the Dutch language, that he
thought and dreamed in it! Often he undertook venture-
some winter journeys to visit the outposts of his flock
beyond the Drakensburg. At Winburg, for example,
there was a very numerous Afrikaans community. On
one of these journeys Lindley confirmed the future President Paul Kruger himself on a farm at Valsch River near
Kroonstad. This tall, bearded, *predikant* was renowned
as a gardener and farmer as well. He first introduced the
seeds of the American seringa tree into Natal, and persuaded his neighbours to grow them. When the calves
died from distended livers (causing by overdrinking their
mothers' milk) and the cows would yield no further milk,
he taught the Boers to make dummy calves by stretching
calf-skins on wooden frames filled with grass. The cows
caught the smell of the counterfeits and yielded their milk
again. Thus, for seven years, he ministered with great
acceptance. It is no wonder that the late Dr. A. Dreyer
described him as the founder (*stigter*) of the Dutch
Reformed Church in Natal, the Orange Free State, and
the Transvaal.

In 1846 the Lieutenant-Governor of Natal appointed
him a member of the Government Commission to advise
on suitable locations or reserves for the 100,000 Zulus in
Natal. He and Theophilus Shepstone were generally to be
found together on the side of the angels in all discussions.
They both supported the view that the Natives in these
locations should be governed as far as possible by their
own tribal laws and customs, and were anxious to provide few but large reserves rather than a multitude of
small locations. Under their guidance the Commission
recommended that training facilities in industry and agri-

culture should be provided in each of the locations. Consideration of economy and the opposition of the farmers alone prevented some of the most far-reaching proposals from coming into effect.

Lindley returned to the American work in Natal after his ministry with the Boers. He was asked to set up a mission station in the new Inanda location, one of the loveliest parts of a lovely province. Here he fell into the ways of a missionary and Jack of all trades again: he was architect and mason, carpenter and plumber, doctor and dentist, magistrate and minister! Coffee and groceries were bought in Durban; for the rest they lived on their own stock and orchard-garden. Distractions were provided in the shape of a leopard hunt (Lindley describes a thrilling encounter with this ' tiger '), or in the persons of distinguished visitors, such as Sir George Grey, Bishop Colenso, or Dr. Alexander Duff. Mrs. Lindley was as active as ever. In addition to all the responsibilities of looking after a large family, she undertook to teach some of the Native girls on the location the rudiments of domestic science. The result was that the eligible Zulu bachelors for miles around sought the hands of ' Mrs. Lindley's girls '.

In May, 1859, it was time for the Lindleys to go on furlough, after twenty-five years of outstanding service to South Africa. He was presented with an inscribed Bible and a purse of 150 guineas from the Colonists. They left with the deep affection of Afrikaners, the English and the Zulus. The three years' furlough was anything but a rest-cure! Lindley spent this time in the U.S.A. as a most successful missionary deputation, and he returned as *Doctor* Daniel Lindley, having received the Doctorate of Divinity of the University of Ohio.

He was back in his beloved Inanda in 1863 and assisted in the foundation of a Zulu girls' seminary there. Soon, at neighbouring Amanzimtoti, the institute for boys and men was founded, which to-day is known throughout South Africa as the Adams College. As a missionary Lindley became more progressive with the years. He believed, for example, that the *uku-lobola* custom (or marriage-dowry of cattle) should be continued, though many missionaries wished to abolish it as a ' heathen ' custom. He urged that it contributed to the stability of marriage and to the respect in which men-folk held their brides. While other missionaries wished to prolong the period of Christian tutelage for the Zulus, Lindley believed the time had come for Zulu pastors of proven merit to be settled in Native congregations. In December 1870 James Dube (a splendid figure of a man, over six feet two inches high and weighing only 200 lb.) was ordained and inducted as minister of the Inanda Church. In his address Lindley declared: ' This is the gladdest day in my life. I never anticipated beholding such a sight as this.' So the days passed all too quickly by. Daniel was now seventy-two years old and had to make arrangements for his final departure from the land of his adoption in 1873. Only the need for expert medical treatment for Lucy, and the clamour of their children and grandchildren in the States, enabled them to tear up their roots. The prospect of an American winter (' Winter that one can *see* ') appalled Lindley. After a farewell visit to their Boer friends in the O.F.S. they left South Africa. Having expended a treasure of sacrificial service, they left with a lifetime's savings amounting to only 500 dollars!

In 1877 Lucy Lindley died, and Daniel could only be persuaded to remain divided from her for three more years. He joined her in 1880. He was a Voortrekker of the Spirit and South Africa is immeasurably his debtor.

CHAPTER VI

ROBERT GRAY

THE Church of the Province of South Africa owes
most under God to Robert Gray who founded it and
fought to gain its spiritual freedom. South Africa was
the land of his adoption and his tired body was laid to
rest in Claremont soil. He came in 1847 to a vast
diocese of more than 200,000 square miles in which there
were over 200 ministers or missionaries of other Christian
Communions but less than a handful of Anglican clergy.
At his death, twenty-five years later, the one diocese had
become six, and the foundations of the seventh (St. John's
Kaffraria) were laid. By the renowned 'Third Proviso'
drawn up by the First Provincial Synod of 1870, in its
Constitution and Canons, the Privy Council was excluded
as a Court of Appeal for the South African Church, and
the last shackles of Church dependence upon the State
(Erastianism) were severed.

The battle for the spiritual independence of the Church
of the Province was to wear out the preternaturally aged
prelate, and to involve him in distasteful controversy.
The first bout was fought with the Rev. William Long
of Mowbray, the prelude to the mightier struggle with
Bishop John William Colenso of Natal, on the issue of
which the sister Anglican Provinces throughout the world
hung. Though gentle of disposition, and an affectionate
father and father-in-God, he was called to brace himself
for a constitutional struggle fought out in the limelight
of the Pan-Anglican Congress, the first of those gatherings
of bishops which later became known as the Lambeth
Conferences. It then seemed that the conservatism of

the English Bench of Bishops (with the almost solitary exception of Wilberforce of Oxford) was matched by the loyalty of his South African clergy and the understanding of the North American bishops who were already emancipated from State interference.

Many, not communicants of the Church of the Province, have cause to remember him gratefully as an educationalist, for the Diocesan College, Rondebosch (affectionately known as ' Bishops '), was his foundation, and this might with more fidelity and accuracy have been known as ' Bishop Gray's '. He also established St. George's Cathedral Grammar School, Cape Town, and was the inspiration of the Cape Town Home and Orphanage dedicated to the patron saint of England. Not least among his many foundations was ' Sunflower ' (Zonnebloem) College for the instruction of African and Coloured in the Christian Faith. It is of interest to recall that the cottages at right-angles to the original Bishopscourt in Protea estate were the home, first of Bishops College, and then of the ' Kaffir College '. It was in the latter that the youth John X. Merriman assisted in the teaching. For these and many other examples of his devotion and foresight this man of God has placed the Church of the Province and the educationalists and philanthropists of the Union in his debt.

Robert Gray was born on 3 October 1809, in the Rectory of Bishopswearmouth in Sunderland. He was the twelfth child and seventh son of a family of fourteen, six of whom fell prey to tuberculosis before Robert reached the age of twenty-two. Spiritually, but not physically, his origin was a blessed one. His father became Bishop of Bristol (in the succession of such a prince of the Church as Butler of *Analogy of Religion* fame), and he had the doubtful benefit of an education at Eton which ended when he was literally trampled on by a crowd of boys emerging from a class-room, so that he had to be wheeled as a cripple in a bath-chair for months afterwards.

His education thereafter was interrupted by illness and the tours on which his father sent him to invigorate his body and broaden his mind. He went to the West Indies, then recommended for chest complaints, with a dying sister, and returned forlorn and alone. In 1828 he went up to University College, Oxford, where he remained until 1831 to share in the excitement of the plans for founding the Oxford Movement, an ecclesiastical revival designed in part to advance the recognition of the Church as the spiritual Body of Christ, and not as a Whitehall Department of State. During this year (1831), when on vacation in Bristol, he saw his father's episcopal palace burnt down by the Radicals who disapproved of the prelate for his opposition to the proposed Reform Bill. In 1834 he was ordained priest in Wells Cathedral, spending much of his time assisting his enfeebled father and reading theology.

At the end of the year he was appointed Rector of Whitworth in the Diocese of Durham, where he worked indefatigably for the next ten years. As there was no Rectory attached to this living, he look lodgings in Durham, but was often invited to stay with the squire at Old Park, Whitworth, whose talented daughter, Sophy Myddleton, he married in 1835. In addition to his pastoral round, be became a tireless secretary of the Society for the Propagation of the Gospel, an Anglican Missionary Society founded in 1701, with a special responsibility for congregations in British dependencies. He and his wife read ecclesiastical history and theology together, and, as a welcome relaxation from these strenuous pursuits, went horse-riding — an unconscious anticipation of their life in the Cape.

Canon Gray (as he was now styled) had been only a short time in his second incumbency at Stockton when he received a letter, dated 30 January 1847, which was to determine the whole trend of his future. It came from the Secretary of the Colonial Bishoprics' Fund asking him to consider the Sees either of Cape Town or Adelaide. An approving reply would be interpreted by his friends as exile for life; for him it was a question of where he could best serve God and whether he was adequate. His concern can be read in his reply: ' I cannot judge for myself whether I am really wanted, but if those over me think so, I am ready cheerfully to go to any post that may be selected for me. . . .' The Archbishop ended the suspense with a definite recommendation in a letter sent in March 1847: ' Being very desirous of finding a priest whose piety, soundness and principles, ability and judgment, would do justice to the Church in this very important station. . . . I am constrained to offer to recommend you for the Cape of Good Hope.'

On St. Peter's Day, 1847, Robert Gray was consecrated the first Bishop of Cape Town in Westminster Abbey. Thereafter, until his arrival in Cape Town on Sunday, 20 February 1848, he was occupied in finding funds and man-power for his diocese. During his lifetime it is claimed that he raised over £130,000 for the Church of the Province. His first impressions of Cape Town are realistic and even prophetic:

I landed in the afternoon with Sophy and Douglas [the ordained son of an Earl] and Douglas read the prayers in the Cathedral in the evening, where there was a tolerable congregation. St. George's is decidedly the best ecclesiastical building in the town. Church matters are in a bad state. I am told there is a party ripe for anything, and full of suspicions and jealousies. . . . I feel the great need there is of judgment, prudence and forebearance, and how much I shall need all your prayers in a very trying and delicate position.

With typical decisiveness the Bishop had within a few weeks decided to rent the Protea estate, seven miles from Cape Town. He was later able to purchase this for £4,000 through the generosity of Miss Burdett Coutts. This estate, formerly known as *Boschheuvel* (Wooded Hill), had probably belonged to Commander Jan van Riebeeck and made a splendid retreat for the energetic Bishop and Mrs. Gray. He was at first apprehensive as to its grandeur, but he contrived to make it a centre of learning as well as a haven of spiritual refreshment for his clergy. Above all it was a home; and the Bishop, who suffered from insomnia due to the cares of the churches, loved to walk among its orchards and shrubs, perhaps ' annihilating all that's made to a green thought in a green shade '. Sophy Gray was the dynamic centre of Bishopscourt, for the Bishop was generally away on some long and arduous itinerary. Here her children were born and brought up; here her green fingers made the garden even lovelier; here she drew and painted; here she kept the accounts and wrote the letters for the absent Bishop; here she entertained the great and the humble. Thence, too, she was happy to escape occasionally on her favourite chestnut ' Bokkie '. We may picture her vividly in Mrs. Brooke's fascinating biography (*Robert Gray, First Bishop of Cape Town*) setting off to accompany her husband on the first part of his visitations:

> Dressed in a dark green plaid dress, with a large grey felt hat, trimmed with an ostrich feather, she accompanied the Bishop on his long exacting journeys through the immense diocese. . . . With her she took her sketch book, pencils and paints, and her delicate little pictures of the country may still be seen. As they went up she painted the little, high-shouldered Gothic churches, which she had designed and which stand to her memory to this day.

Although the Bishop had difficulties, he also had stalwart friends. They included Archdeacon Merriman (whom

he termed 'my Archdeacon Merriman') and the Rev.
H. M. White, Fellow of New College, Oxford, who came
out as first Head of the Diocesan College. In the spring
of 1848 he started on his first visitation and was away
for four months, travelling eastward. When at Grahamstown, he learned that the Governor was meeting a group
of Bantu chiefs at Kingswilliamstown. Immediately he
set off and completed the ninety miles, including the
fording of a flooded river, in a day. It seems that he
was disappointed with this encounter, since he observes
that the chiefs, when invited to accept missionaries, stated
a decided preference for blankets, tiger-skins and brandy!

His second visitation was to St. Helena; and his third,
probably the most remarkable of all, took him a journey
of 4,000 miles which he completed in nine months. He
rode through the Cape Colony and through the Orange
River Sovereignty down to Natal, returning through
Kaffraria to the Cape. He set out on Easter Monday,
sending word that he hoped to reach Pietermaritzburg by
Whitsunday. In fact, he arrived there on the eve of
Pentecost, after riding 1,400 miles in seven weeks. This
visitation is a tribute to his pioneering courage and perseverance. He deserved to be known as 'the post-cart
Bishop'.

In 1852 he returned to England, partly to raise more
funds, but also to arrange for the sub-division of his vast
diocese into the dioceses of Grahamstown and Natal. On
St. Andrew's Day, 1853, he assisted in the consecration
of Armstrong and Colenso as Bishops. It is this day,
incidentally, that is commemorated in the name of St.
Andrew's College in Grahamstown, whose founder was
Bishop Armstrong. During his absence from the Cape
Bishop Gray preached over three hundred sermons com-
mending to the parishes of England the work so dear to
his heart.

On his return the work went happily until 1861, although there were murmurings from Natal. In that year the incumbent of St. Peter's, Mowbray, refused to attend the Diocesan Synod which the Bishop was convening. Mr. Long opposed the step as an infraction of English law. Of this and similiar episodes, Mrs. Brooke says, with justifiable mordancy, ' It was as if, for some people, the first commandment was now, " Thou shalt worship the Law thy God ".' The Privy Council upheld Long's contention, and the Bishop had to re-instate him.

The energies of Bishop Gray were now devoted to the extension of the work of the Church. The Diocese of St. Helena had been founded in 1859, and in 1863 Edward Twells was consecrated as the first Bishop of the Orange Free State. Earlier, Bishop Gray had assisted Livingstone in the founding of the missionary episcopate of Central Africa, where Bishop Mackenzie met an untimely but heroic end.

Much of the Bishop's time was taken up in controversy not of his choosing, in particular the drawn-out struggle of orthodox doctrine and ecclesiastical independence versus heterodoxy and Erastianism. Gray was the protagonist of the former view, Colenso of the latter. Though, in fairness to Colenso, it must be admitted that he had an acute mind and a deep missionary compassion for the Zulus, none the less, it was sad that so much of the time of the 'Athanasius of the South ' (as his admirers styled the Metropolitan in their enthusiasm) had to be spent in combat with Erastianism in high places.

His exhausing work, however, was nearly completed in 1870 when the historic first Provincial Synod was held. After producing her Magna Charta the Church of the Province could, under the Headship of her Lord, manage her own affairs. A year later another dream was fulfilled in the foundation of St. Cyprian's School for girls. The same year, alas, was marked by the sorrow of losing his beloved companion and wife, Sophy ('my chiefest of many blessings'). For a year he lived 'divided with but half a heart, Till we shall meet and never part' (to use the words of another Bishop a century before him). Then the tired body of Robert Gray was laid beside her in the shadow of St. Saviour's, Claremont, a church which she had designed. But there was nothing here for tears, for a holy man, a lover of all sorts and conditions of men, and the architect of the Church of the Province of South Africa had joined the Church Triumphant.

CHAPTER VII

EUGÈNE CASALIS

IT has been said that the French Reformed mission in Basutoland is not so much an ecclesiastical institution, as a family association. The constant reappearance of such names as Casalis, Mabille, Pelissier, Dyke and Rolland, among others, in the histories of Basutoland is a remarkable testimony to the contributions that families, rather than individuals, have made to the moral and cultural elevation of the Basuto. It is also an embarrassment to the biographer to select one individual of one family for inclusion in this series. The choice of Eugène Casalis, senior, has been made because he was one of the three pioneer missionaries to Basutoland; because his eminence was recognized by the Paris Evangelical Missionary Society in recalling him after twenty-three years of service to be the Director of its missionary training in Paris; because his travels have been graphically recounted in two volumes, entitled *Mes Souvenirs* and *Les Bassoutos;* and, not least, because the family tradition was continued in the work of his son, Eugène, and his daughter, Adèle, who married the great consolidator of his pioneering work, Adolphe Mabille. Furthermore, by his marriage to Sarah Dyke, Eugène senior was linked to another family which did signal service in the French Reformed Church in Basutoland.

Eugène Casalis came of Huguenot stock and traditions. He was born in 1812 at Orthez, in the South of France. His mother was the daughter of a distinguished patroness and custodian of persecuted Huguenot ministers, and Segalas (the mansion where Eugène was born and where he was to spend so many of his early years) was a renowned refuge for Huguenots. A sickly child, dropped on his head by a careless nurse when only two, it is remarkable that he lived at all, and almost incredible that he should have been a pioneer missionary for twenty-three years, and that he died at the age of seventy-nine. His upbringing seems to have been strictly conventional and orthodox, though it had its merry moments, as when he acted as valet to his grandfather, or heard his grandmother relate how she had outwitted the long arm of the law. Eugène relates one example:

One day when her husband and a minister were conferring about the interests of the faithful of Bearn, a breathless peasant announced that the dragoons were near. She gave the alarm and closing the gate of the house, sat quietly in front of it, sewing. The detachment arrived, the officer-in-charge demanding peremptorily an entry. She, without a trace of emotion, placed her hand on the latch and replied, ' Sir, I will not open until you show me your orders.' The captain fortunately had forgotten them, or had thought it unnecessary to bring them, ground his teeth, threatened, then acknowledging the superiority of a lady who dared to remind armed men of the inviolability of her home, muttered some miserable excuses. Meantime, the minister and his friend had escaped by the small window which overlooked the vines, and thence they had reached the woods. Believing them to be already far away, my grandmother raised the latch and said, ' Sir, if my gate is closed to anyone who threatens to force it, without the royal authority, it is open to those who, like yourselves, need refreshment and rest.'

To live with such a grandmother was itself an education in courage and Christian convictions. In later years, however, Eugène felt that he had perhaps learned more of the fear than of the love of God in his earliest years.

The beginning of his vocation as a missionary can be traced in his ninth year. He had, he tells us, at that age a ' living sympathy ' for any negro or mulatto whom he saw, greatly to the embarrassment of some of the friends of the family. He attributed this sentiment to two histories and a missionary pamphlet that he read. He felt ' a living pity for the American Indians in reading a history of the conquest of Mexico and that of Peru '. He was equally moved by a missionary novelette, entitled *Gumal and Lina*, and, in particular, by an engraving of Gumal, an African boy, who was shown lifting his arms to the sky after his baptism, exclaiming amid the solitude of the forests, ' I am a Christian!' The remarkable fact is that this compassion was to deepen with the years, and to be allied to a fortitude of purpose.

A year later he went to Bayonne to be under the supervision of a Reformed minister, charged with giving him an introduction to the classics. He learned Greek and Latin in a hard school. He was given an exercise book, told to fill the first half of it with declensions and conjugations, and the latter part with translations. When this was done, his reward would be a glimpse of Biarritz and the ocean. His spiritual life was deepened at this time by a careful translation and analysis of the *Epistle to the Romans*, the very book that awakened the souls of leaders as various as Augustine of Hippo, Martin Luther, John Wesley and Karl Barth, all in the epistolary succession. M. Pyt, his friend and tutor, kept his compassion alive by taking him on pastoral visitations of the prison-inmates and the poor of Bayonne. His most vivid memory was their joint discovery of an unhappy woman and her daughter, so poverty-stricken that they had only one dress between them. When one left the house wearing their only dress, the other remained in bed hidden under a cotton bed-cover.

Though his tutor and his parents urged him to reconsider his decision to be a missionary, his determination was inflexible. In 1830 he was sent to the Mission House of

the Paris Evangelical Missionary Society to receive training. There he and his confrères received a most compre-
hensive training, using to the full the resources of the
University, where they attended the lectures given both
in the Sorbonne and the Collège de France. Eugène
proudly remembers that he once assisted the great Cuvier
in his famous reconstruction of prehistoric animals, and
that he heard Champollion lecture on Egyptian hiero-
glyphics. Apart from the varied lectures they attended,
and the famous preachers (such as Monod) whom they
heard, and the formal instruction given at the Mission
House on theology and missions, their vocation was tested
in the open-air preaching in the down-town parts of the
great city, near the Sèvres barricade. ' In this villainous
quarter ', he says, ' where mountebanks and charlatans of
every type flourished, we prepared for our future sermons
among the savages. It was a good school; for sheer din
and discord none of the tomtoms which I have heard in
Africa could rival the cymbals and tambourins of the
strolling Parisian players.' But even this noise had its
compensations: it convened a congregation and exercised
the vocal powers of the future missionaries to the full.

His training was completed in 1832, and he prepared
with his comrade, Arbousset, and an older artisan missionary named Gosselin, to leave France for England, thence to
sail to the Cape. Leave-taking was most poignant,
because at this time few people expected to see a pioneer
missionary to the dark continent ever return alive. Such
of his friends as wished him *Au revoir,* muttered under
their breath, ' in heaven!'

The three musketeers of the Spirit, as these gay comrades in the work of Christ might be termed, embarked
at Gravesend (port of the ominous name!) on the *Test,*
an English barque of 250 tons, which took over three-
and-a-half months to reach the Cape. For relaxation on
the voyage Arbousset and he undertook to summarize a

text-book of four volumes, each a hundred pages in length, on surgery and medicine. After a severe storm they reached the Cape on 24 February 1833, where they were welcomed by friends of Dr. Philip. At that time Dr. Philip's championship of the cause of the Hottentots caused him to be the butt of many Cape Town citizens, who paid the criers of fish to hawk the most evil-smelling of their wares under his windows. None the less, the French missionaries were impressed by their redoubtable host. And it was Dr. Philip who suggested the Basuto as the nation which the missionaries should evangelize. They received this recommendation with all the more avidity as he had to tell them of the misfortune that had followed their French predecessors, Lemue, Rolland and Pelissier, who had been forced to give up their work when Mzilikazi's hordes had scattered the Bahurutse among whom they were labouring.

Having bought provisions and equipment the three friends started on the journey that was to lead them to the Basuto. In days when mission stations, manses and farmsteads were the only hotels, they were glad to rest their tired limbs in Bethelsdorp or share the copious meals at the *Pastorie* in Graaff-Reinet. Casalis had the unfortunate experience, through breaking his spectacles, of mistaking a gnu for a lion a few miles from the ' gem of the Karroo '. But hardships were not all imaginary, and he and his companions (who included Hottentots and Krotz, the interpreter) were frequently awakened by jackals, leopards and lions.

The first view of their future charges was obtained in the neighbourhood of Thaba Nchu (the Black Mountain) where they were led to Moseme, a sub-chief of the paramount chieftain, Moshesh. After being well received by him they made arrangements to hold a service the next morning, at which Moseme and a hundred of his tribe were present. Casalis preached the first missionary sermon in this neighbourhood, its simple theme being that the missionaries served a heavenly Father who had revealed Himself to them, and whose blessings they were bringing to the Basuto. Casalis later could remember only one sentence in his sermon, because of its local colour. It went thus: 'If you will receive our message, you will be like the ostrich which rejects its old feathers in order to get more beautiful ones.'

The missionaries, like every sensitive traveller after them, were stupefied by the view from Moseme's place. They remarked on the magnificence of a panorama which showed majestic mountain ranges, each mountain like a fortress, with its peak circled with a gigantic granite necklace of rocks, while below vast plateaux seemed to beckon flocks and herds to pasture there. In the far distance, they dimly discerned a grey peak, Thaba Bosiu (a Mountain by Night), where, they were told, the paramount chief Moshesh lived, surrounded by his warriors on an impregnable height.

Soon they were to see Thaba Bosiu for themselves and to be the first white men to parley with Moshesh. Thaba Bosiu, among the Malutis, is a five-sided mountain, whose plateau of a peak seems almost as wide at its base. From the plain where they stood they were able to make out a vast number of black dots from the middle of which smoke appeared; these were the huts of the vast concourse of Moshesh's people. There seemed to be only one way of scaling this natural citadel, and that was by a steep ravine. This they ascended, holding their horses by their bridles. On reaching the level of the plateau they were met by a salute of muskets fired in the air, a rather ferocious form of greeting. Next they were met by a strange figure who combined the offices of herald, jester and chief-of-police to Moshesh. This grotesque apparition seemed to be earning his nickname as 'Dog of the town', for the curious Basuto recoiled before his shrieks, leaving a semi-circle in the midst of which Moshesh was seated in state.

This figure, whom Prof. J. du Plessis describes ambivalently as ' the ablest politician which the Bantu race has yet produced ', was clearly a man of intelligence and strength of will, for he had welded the tribes into a remarkable unity under his authority. Casalis was impressed. He wrote: ' I knew immediately that I had to do with a superior man, accustomed to thinking, to commanding others, and, above all, to commanding himself.' He seemed about forty-five years of age, well-made, without any signs of obesity. He was wearing, a little negligently, a large kaross of panther-skins, which covered his knees and feet. His only ornaments were a fillet of beads on his forehead, from which there hung a tuft of feathers, an ivory bracelet which he wore on his right arm, as a symbol of authority, and several copper rings on his wrists.

The missionaries were also taken to meet his chief wife, and on the following day they explained their business to Moshesh. They told him how perturbed they were to learn of the unhappy conditions of the chief's people (they had seen whitening bones of his slaughtered subjects recently), and they believed they had a sovereign remedy for all their evils, which they strongly urged him to try. The evils of the Basuto came from their passions and their ignorance, but the missionaries, as emissaries of a God of peace, wished to bring to the chief's people the blessings of order, tranquillity and prosperity. If Moshesh and his subjects would be guided by the missionaries, he would inaugurate a new era of happiness, under the influence of the new beliefs and customs they would introduce. As a proof of their sincerity they offered to establish themselves in the middle of the Basuto, and to share the life of the people. They asked for a place where they might

build houses and dig plantations, which would serve as
models for the Natives.

Moshesh gave this permission readily, and the first
station, Morija, which is even to-day the headquarters
of the French Reformed mission in Basutoland, was built.
It was named Morija to commemorate the providential
guidance by which the three friends had been led, on
9 July 1833.

The eldest of the three comrades, Gosselin, was the
director of building operations, and his invincible good-
humour seemed as valuable as his technical qualifications.
Eugène Casalis did not take too readily to the felling and
sawing of trees, or the breaking and shaping of stones;
but, whether they liked it or not, the work went with a
will.   Arbousset seems to have been an activist, and the
more meditative Casalis fell more easily a prey to melancholy.   Casalis was, of course, in his early twenties and
so was often seized by homesickness.   The jolly Gosselin
cured him of this by digging a grave and, with a
solemn face, suggesting that Casalis should be interred
as the excavated area was a perfect fit!

The first buildings completed, they now turned to
agriculture and animal husbandry. Cereals, vegetables,
peaches, apricots and figs were planted. Superior breeds
of dog were produced, and ducks and geese were introduced. The Basuto were most astonished by the attention the missionaries gave to raising pigs, which were to
them the most filthy and undiscriminating of animals —
they even ate snakes!   On the other hand, cats, which
they met for the first time, seemed a gift from heaven,
for their huts were infested with mice and rats and they
could not find a way to get rid of them.   Casalis avers
that they would almost have worshipped this ' miniature
leopard ' with the noiseless tread.   The missionaries had
a most catholic taste in animals: they brought up a tame
zebra and almost managed to domesticate a gnu!

Other stations were being founded by their predecessors in Africa, Pelissier, who established Bethulie on the Orange River, and Rolland, who founded Beersheba on the Caledon. At a conference of all the French missionaries, it was decided that one of their number should establish a station in the immediate neighbourhood of the paramount chief, below Thaba Bosiu. Eugène Casalis was selected for this task.

He and Gosselin started to build the missionary's cabin, when torrential rains forced Gosselin to return to Morija to save some bricks which he had left drying in the sun. The lonely and woe-begone Casalis was left alone to his reflections. It was then that he began to think most seriously of marriage. He records that the sight of his unmended clothes advertised his matrimonial need. The need for further missionary equipment and for a companion in his solitude found him making the long journey back to Cape Town via Bethelsdorp, Hankey, Pacaltsdorp and Genadendal. After a careful observance of his future wife's demeanour and habits, during a six weeks stay in the Cape, ardour overcame caution, and he married Sarah Dyke on 13 April 1836. They seem to have been ideally matched, and it must have given Eugène great pleasure when his own son, Eugène junior, went to the Basuto mission in 1858, two years after the father had returned to Paris to direct the parent society.

The courage and the adaptability of pioneer missionaries is a commonplace of missionary history. What is not, perhaps, equally realized is the difficulty of sustaining faith, hope, patience, culture and compassion among a primitive people. Casalis tells us how these difficulties were overcome. ' The intellectual side of our nature was safeguarded by the varied observations of all kinds that we made, by the study of the native language, and by the refreshment we procured in reading French, Latin and other classics.' The religious side of their nature hardly suffered at all, because of 'the daily experience which we had of the protection of God and the gentle visitations of his Spirit'. But, most of all, were they sustained by the thought that they were ambassadors of Christ in places which were completely barricaded against the entry of the Gospel until they came. He was able to say, 'None of us experienced even the shadow of a regret for having left all that was most dear to us for the Lord'.

Other missions were to be established afterwards, the Roman Catholics commencing twenty-nine years after the French Reformed mission, and the Church of the Province of South Africa forty-three years later. But it was Eugène Casalis and his compatriots who endured the first hardships, built the first mission stations with their bare hands out of granite, and taught the Basuto agriculture and husbandry, and, above all, gave them the unsearchable riches of Christ. In Eugène Casalis, we salute a pioneer missionary and linguist; a patriarch, author and statesman, who was known in his day and lives in the traditions of the Basuto folk as *Mahloana-Matsoana* ('The man with the small black eyes') and the 'friend of Moshesh'.

CHAPTER VIII

DAVID LIVINGSTONE THE MISSIONARY

L IVINGSTONE spent only eleven years as a missionary within the confines of the area now known as the Union of South Africa and the Protectorates, but they were the formative years of his life and he learned his medical, missionary and exploratory apprenticeship in South Africa. He was probably the most distinguished missionary in history, with the single exception of Saint Paul. As an explorer he was world-renowned, adding the Victoria Falls, and Lakes Ngami, Nyasa and Bangweulu to the map of Africa. He was, moreover, the first European to make the Trans-African crossing from West to Eastern coasts (Loanda to Quilimane). He was, further, an author with a world-wide reading public. His *Missionary Travels*, for example, ran through fourteen editions and sold 70,000 copies. He was honoured by the Royal Geographical Society with its gold medal and by the Cities of London and Glasgow by the award of their Freedom to him. His greatest honour, one that is given only to the outstanding figures and benefactors of the nation, was his burial in the national shrine of Westminster Abbey. The magnetism of his friendship drew to him the affectionate admiration of leaders in the realms of politics, science, missions and big-game hunting. Sir Roderick Murchison (President of the Geographical Society), Dr. Risdon Bennett (President of the Royal College of Physicians), Sir Thomas Maclear (Astronomer Royal at the Cape), Oswell the hunter and explorer, as well as the Queen herself and Mr. Gladstone, delighted to honour him, as did Sir George Grey, the Governor of the Cape. His was a name more distinguished than any ever associated with Africa and the title which he rejoiced in most was the unassuming one of ' missionary '.

It is not surprising, therefore, that he enjoyed an almost legendary reputation among Africans. One of them met Bishop Chancey Maples on the higher reaches of the Rovuma River and presented the Bishop with a blue serge coat, which he valued as if it were a saint's relic. He said that it had been given him ten years before by Livingstone. He described the donor thus: ' A man who treated black men as brothers and whose memory would be cherished along the Rovuma after we are all dead. A short man with a keen, piercing eye, whose words were always gentle and whose manners were always kind, whom as a leader it was a privilege to follow, and who knew the way to the heart of all men.' That must be one of the greatest unsolicited testimonials in all history!

Our interest in this essay is limited to Livingstone as a missionary and humanitarian in South Africa. This was, after all, his greatest work. Many have explored Africa, though none so venturously or indefatigably as he, but he was supreme in his exploration of the African mind and in evoking the trust, the loyalty and the admiration of his dark-skinned brethren.

Livingstone's origins and choice of career were curiously like those of his father-in-law, Dr. Robert Moffat. Both came of humble but independent Scots stock. Both had to work long hours at an early age, Moffat as a gardener, Livingstone as a piecer (one who tied the broken threads of the yarn together) in a spinning-mill. Each had a rudimentary education and studied at night school after working-hours. Each, by a strange coincidence, won the esteem of his comrades by a rescue from drowning. Each offered himself to the London Missionary Society as a missionary, though Livingstone's first choice was China, and he accepted Africa as a second-best.

Each believed that a missionary should be a pioneer, not a man who steps into the safe shoes of another. Each had the brave spirit which meets the heads of African tribes, notorious for their bloodthirstiness, unafraid. Each began his career in the Northern Cape and Bechuanaland. They were united by ties of admiration and by the marriage of Mary Moffat with David Livingstone. Each, too, had revolted against the chill Calvinism he inherited, refusing to believe that God predestined some to salvation and others to irremediable damnation, though each retained his Calvinist sense of being the chosen agent of God to work for His Glory on the mission field. Each, too, believed that Christianity must be accompanied by the civilizing power of education and vocational training. Each, also, was a superb linguist. The main difference between them was that Moffat was an artisan missionary, Livingstone a medical missionary.

Livingstone first reached the Cape on 15 March 1840. The first important personality he met was Dr. John Philip. The younger man was prejudiced against Philip, being inclined to believe that he was an agitator and a martinet to his colleagues. He left Philip, as so many others, convinced of the integrity and splendid courage of the man. Indeed, in Livingstone's lifelong attack on the slave-traders, he seems to have inherited Philip's role, as John Mackenzie inherited Livingstone's, as champion of the Coloured peoples.

It is altogether fitting that Dr. James Macnair calls his biography, the most recent, *Livingstone the Liberator*, for as missionary, as explorer and as medical man, his single aim was to liberate men from the thraldom, respectively, of egotism, exploitation and disease. That title links all his diverse activities.

When Livingstone reached Kuruman he was impatient of the tardiness of Moffat's arrival, so he and an artisan colleague named Edwards started on a northward trek to seek for more suitable mission sites. They first chose Lepelole in the territory of the Bakwena. Livingstone, once the chief had welcomed them, decided with a characteristic thoroughness to stay on alone in this station in order to learn the language and the customs of the African tribe from the Africans themselves, without any European intermediary. He undoubtedly had a gift for discovering the African. Professor Coupland, probably the greatest living authority on Livingstone, writes: ' It is clear that he had a peculiar gift for seeing what lay at the back of the native mind. Irrational suspicions, mysterious motives, ridiculous arguments, he could understand and deal with them all.'

His first two years were thus an apprenticeship — he had learned of African customs and the Tswana tongue. But even at this early stage in his career, his dogged determination of character is revealed. 'Some of my companions', so he wrote, ' who had recently joined us and did not know that I understood a little of their speech, were overheard by me discussing my appearance and powers. He is not strong. He is quite thin. He only appears stout because he puts himself into those bags (trousers!).'

He added, ' This caused my Highland blood to rise and made me disguise my fatigue by keeping them all at top speed for days, until I heard them expressing proper opinion of my pedestrian powers.' Moreover, it was during this time that he first saw slavery ('open sore of Africa ') and he vowed to strike at it with all the strength he possessed.

In July 1843 permission was given to establish a forward mission station. As the chief of the Bakwena had died, as the result of an explosive present sent by another chief, they decided to move to Mobatsa, with Sechele, chief of the related tribe of the Bakhatla. Livingstone had gained the chief's admiration by curing his only son of a critical

illness. He was the missionary's first convert, baptized
after five years of preliminary instruction. Apart from a
temporary lapse from grace, he was remarkably constant,
enduring the accusation of disloyalty on the part of his
tribe, for forsaking their ancient beliefs and customs for
the Christian life. It was at Mobatsa that Livingstone
had the famous encounter with the lion, which perma-
nently injured his arm. Apparently, Livingstone shot at
the beast from a distance of thirty yards. The king of
beasts then bounded straight at him over an intervening
bush. Of this literally face-to-face encounter, the missionary wrote:

> I saw the lion just in the act of springing upon me. I
> was upon a little height; he caught my shoulder as he sprang,
> and we both came to the ground below together. Growling
> horribly close to my ear, he shook me as a terrier dog does a
> rat. The shock produced a stupor similar to that which seems
> to be felt by a mouse after the first shake of the cat. It
> caused a sort of dreariness, in which there was no sense of
> pain nor feeling of terror, though quite conscious of all that
> was happening. . . . The shake annihilated fear, and
> allowed no sense of horror in looking round at the beast.
> This peculiar state is probably produced in all animals killed
> by the carnivora; and if so, is a merciful provision by our
> benevolent Creator for lessening the pain of death.

An African teacher then fired twice at the beast and
distracted his attention from Livingstone, whilst the spear
of a third African despatched the lion.

One happy result of this misfortune was his convales-
cence at Kuruman and subsequent marriage to Mary
Moffat. The man who refused to capitulate to the lion,
was captivated by this lamb! Livingstone can hardly
have been a gallant lover, for he describes his new bride
in a private letter as ' a not romantic but matter-of-fact
lady, a little, thick, black-haired girl and all I want'.
Though Livingstone's long absences from home, while ex-

ploring the African hinterland, were to make her married life lonely and responsible, she would not have exchanged her bridegroom for any other.

Their first home together was at Mobatsa, but it soon had to be broken up because Livingstone found it impossible to work under an artisan missionary who was eighteen years his senior and regarded suggestions as criticisms. Livingstone decided to move on, even though this meant building a new house and the additional expenditure could ill be spared on an income of £100 per annum.

They now moved on to Chonuana, forty miles to the north in the Bakwena territory. Here he had a famous encounter and conversation with a rain-maker, which is most remarkable for the insight Livingstone shows into the Native mind as also for his sense of justice to an opponent. It is typical of his magnanimity that, although a qualified physician and surgeon, instead of condemning medicine-men out of hand, he gave them more scientific suggestions for effecting cures. Moreover, he gave them these medical tips *in camera* so that they would not lose face among their own people. Livingstone was frequently amazed at the capacity of the African for enduring pain. 'Both men and women submit to an operation without wincing, or any of that shouting which caused young students to faint in the operating theatre before the introduction of chloroform.' But even in Chonuana they were to have no abiding place — the fear of drought and punitive raids by the Boers against the Bakwena drove them northward again. Finally, they settled at Kolobeng on the eastern edge of the Kalahari desert, where they lived for five years, the nearest approach to complete contentment Livingstone was ever to know. The mission house was erected on a sandstone eminence overlooking the river, and the missionary often recalled the beauty of its situation and happy associations in later life.

He was now a thoroughly versatile pioneer missionary. He writes that their house was

the third which I had reared with my own hands. A native smith taught me to weld iron; and having improved by scraps of information in that line from Mr. Moffat and also in carpentering and gardening, I was becoming handy at almost any trade, besides doctoring and preaching; and as my wife could make candles, soap and clothes, we came nearly up to what may be considered indispensable in the accomplishments of a missionary family in Central Africa, namely, the husband to be jack of all trades without doors, and the wife a maid-of-all-work within.

There is no doubt that he was happy, if tired, performing the work of a settled missionary. In 1848 he describes a typical day of his work and his wife's:

We get up generally with the sun; then have family worship, breakfast and school, and as soon as these are over we begin the normal operations needed, sawing, ploughing, smithy work.

Meanwhile it appears that Mrs. Livingstone is

employed all morning in culinary and other work and feels pretty tired by dinner-time. We take an hour of rest then, but more frequently . . . she goes off to hold infant school. . . . My manual labour continues till five o'clock I then go into the town to give lessons and talk to any who may be disposed for it. As soon as the cows are milked we have a meeting — this is followed by a prayer-meeting in Sechele's house, which brings me home at half-past eight and generally tired enough — too fatigued to think of any mental exertion.

Livingstone found it desirable to use his medical skill sparingly: otherwise his administrative, pastoral and educational duties would have been smothered by the demands for his services as a physician.

He declares that an undeserved reputation for obstetrical skill became quite embarrassing for him. It all arose from a woman, on whom he performed a slight operation for barrenness, after the Native doctors had failed with the case. She returned to her husband and within a year had presented him with a son. 'The consequence was', he wrote, ' that I was teased with applications from husbands and wives from all parts of the country.' These came distances as great as two hundred miles to procure the precious ' child medicine '. He was, of course, ready to use his professional skill in cases of real urgency, but refused to be deflected from his primary task — the proclamation of the Christian faith.

He had the patience and understanding necessary for his task, and a saving sense of humour. He laughingly describes how the Makololo women behaved at worship. Apparently, those who had children bent down over them in prayer, and the children ' in terror of being crushed to death, set up a simultaneous yell, which so tickled the whole assembly that there was often a subdued titter, to be turned into a hearty laugh as soon as they heard Amen '. It was long before the art of worship and of reverence could be instilled into the missionary's adult charges. He says that often a serious appeal in a sermon would be lost by the loud interjection of one woman, who might notice another sitting on part of her dress, in the words: ' Take the nasty thing away, will you?' Then other neighbours would take sides in the fray, and the men would swear at them all to enforce silence! Such *minutiae*, irritating or amusing (if the missionary was tolerant and understanding), made up a good part of missionary life.

The more Livingstone came into contact with paganism in his pioneering work, the more impressed was he by the benefits Christianity and education had given the evangelized Natives to the south. He adds, prophetically, ' The indirect benefits, which to a casual observer lie beneath the surface and are inappreciable, in reference to the probable wide diffusion of Christianity at some future time, are worth all the money and labour that have been expended to produce them.'

His mind was increasingly turning to the north, as desiccation was already worsening the territory in the environs of Kolobeng. He believed that the Bantu would not be able to resist the continuous white pressure from the south and he was anxious to carry the Gospel and conquer the slave-trade in the interior of Central Africa. He was fired with this desire the more urgently by the timely visit of big-game hunters to his station. Three of them, Steele, Webb and Oswell, who helped to finance his exploratory expeditions, were to be among his pall-bearers in the Westminster Abbey burial a quarter of a century later. The first became a General; the second Livingstone cured of an almost mortal fever, finding him exhausted some miles from the station, and the third was to become his bosom friend. They all warmed, men of the world as they were, to the courage and manliness of this servant of God.

In June 1849 he set out with Mungo Murray and Cotton Oswell to seek for Lake Ngami and thus set his foot on the first rung of the ladder of fame. This was a hard, waterless route to take. Well might he say of this Sahara of the south, 'The pleasantest music in Africa is that made by merry frogs.' At length they came to Lake Ngami, now a flat grass-land.

This discovery set Livingstone thinking of others and made him ambitious to open up a navigable highway through Central Africa as a water-path for Christianity, civilization and commerce. The discovery also made him famous overnight and procured the award of a prize, presented by Queen Victoria, on the recommendation of the Royal Geographical Society.

Two years later, still determined to find a central waterway, he discovered the Upper Zambezi and with this discovery came the full shock of realizing the extent and the dastardly exploitation of the slave-trade. When he returned to Kolobeng it was evident that his family could no longer live in the drought-stricken area. Moreover, he was now preparing to make the great trans-African coast-to-coast journey. His home life and his life as a settled missionary came to an end with the sending of his wife and family to England. Thereafter he was a wanderer, but wherever he went he carried the Gospel and the spirit of brotherhood. Livingstone had won his spurs in South Africa and the knight dedicated to the conquest of slavery was now ready for his long and arduous explorations and struggles against unfriendly men and implacable Nature.

Henceforth the continent claims him and the world acclaims his discoveries. But his apprenticeship and his first triumphs had been gained on the soil of Southern Africa and there he found the greatest happiness in the five contented years at Kolobeng. Thereafter the road led to fame, but also to loneliness and tragedy.

CHAPTER IX

DAVID LIVINGSTONE, THE MAN

THE penalty of greatness is the inquisitiveness of the public and the denigration of the biographer whose miry fingers infallibly detect the clay feet of the public idol. Livingstone, happily, was not caricatured by Lytton Strachey, like the other great Victorians. The nobility of his altruistic penetration of Africa in the interests of Christianity, civilization and honest commerce, remains unquestioned, even after his diaries and correspondence have been subjected to minute scrutiny. Not, of course, that the ' outsize missionary ' and explorer was without foibles and endearing eccentricities. He was a man: he did not pretend to be a hero or a demi-god.

Recent research has, however, brought to light some interesting facts about the man, David Livingstone. How many readers know, for example, that his spelling was atrocious, or that this supposedly inflexible paragon of virtue poached salmon in his youth? Or, that the indomitable explorer was terrified and tongue-tied when he preached his first sermon? Is it generally known that he wrote one of the strongest letters to a mother-in-law that have ever been penned — so virulent that he must have regretted the folly of ever committing his thoughts to paper? How many have heard of his eccentricities of dress, or of the tragedy of his eldest son Robert who threw over completely the parental authority and whose name the younger members of the family were forbidden to mention? Is it known that he had a broken romance with Catherine Ridley before he had even met Mary Moffat?

Apart from these human details, there are many questions to which it is now possible to give at least tentative answers. Livingstone is renowned as Africa's greatest missionary, but what were the beliefs that sustained his heroic pilgrimage? Is it true that, although he revelled in the beauties of Nature (as his famous description of Victoria Falls shows), he was an artistic Philistine and tone-deaf? Did he shun or seek publicity? Did the explorer strangle the missionary in him? Was he inconsiderate to his wife, the woman whom Aloysius Horn described as dragged across Africa by Livingstone?

The new facts, to which I have referred, are conclusively proven. Livingstone's letter of application for acceptance as an agent of the London Missionary Society, although carefully penned, reveals that the words ' God ' and 'Jesus ' were spelled without capital letters and spelling errors are frequent. Curiously enough, considering the accuracy of his scientific observations, he was an inconsistent speller throughout his life.

As to his poaching, the story goes as follows. He once caught a salmon on a prohibited reach of water. Because he could find no other way of concealing his catch, he thrust it down his brother's trousers, and David enjoyed the joke hugely when the villagers sympathized with the swollen limb of his brother, who came limping home. Dour, as he might seem, there was a warning twinkle in Livingstone's eye.

When, in a public address he had recounted the story of his escape from the lion, an earnest questioner asked him what his thoughts were when on the brink of eternity, he answered, ' I was wondering which part of me he was going to eat next '. Incidentally, a privilege that his children enjoyed was being shown the lion's teeth-marks in their father's arm!

It seems that he preached his first sermon in the Congregational Church in Stanford Rivers, in place of the regular minister who was ill. He had committed his sermon to memory, and he began by reading the next out slowly and deliberately.   There was a long, embarrassing pause, after which he blurted out an apology, ' Friends, I have forgotten all I had to say ', and without more ado, the preacher hurried down the pulpit stairs and rushed into the street to cover his confusion.   How different was the first sermon he preached in Cape Town!   If anything, he said too much on this occasion.   It was in the Union Chapel, Cape Town, where his host, Dr. John Philip, was minister.   Livingstone was disturbed by the congregation's lack of support for Dr. Philip's championship of the Coloured races.   He told them so in round terms and succeeded in embarrassing both them and his host!

The regretted letter to his mother-in-law arose from the following circumstances.   Livingstone proposed in 1851 to find a healthy mission site in the Makololo territory, to establish his family there, and thence to set out on a long reconnaissance of routes to the West and East Coasts. Mrs. Moffat was thinking of the inevitable loneliness in store for her daughter and remonstrated, exercising a mother-in-law's privileges to the full.   Livingstone went far beyond a son-in-law's privileges when he replied, ' I have occasionally met with people who took upon themselves to act for me and have offered their thoughts with an emphatic, " I think ", but I generally excuse them on the score of being a little soft-headed in believing that they could think both for me and themselves.'

Livingstone seems to have been a trifle vain in the matter of dress.   This was probably due to his first contact with affluent big-game hunters.   In a letter to Henry Drummond, his Glasgow tailor, he issues the following instruction:

For jackets, I should like something that my good lady calls *respectable* and which, though I can catch the idea, I cannot describe.   We have gentlemen from India, occasionally as visitors, and others, as officers from the Army, coming up, on hunting expeditions.   Now it sounds rather discordant when we hear the title ' Doctor ' applied to a poor fellow in a fustian jacket (i.e. made of coarse cotton fabric mixed with corduroy and moleskin).

His most distinctive article of clothing was his gold-braided cap made in the style of a naval officer's headgear. This is usually, but wrongly, described as his ' Consul's Cap '. Wrongly, because he wore this type of cap before he was appointed Her Majesty's Consul at Quilimane. In Africa the cap had two undoubted advantages: it was stuffed with wadding and offered excellent protection from the sun; and it impressed Arab traders and African chiefs as a symbol of authority. In England, however, where he continued to wear it when on leave, it was an eccentricity, possible deliberately cultivated as a mark of distinction.

Yet, strangely, he was a shy and diffident man. He often hesitated to appear in the London streets, lest he should be mobbed by the inquisitive. Once, indeed, he hastily summoned a cab in Regent Street to escape from the unbridled curiosity of the bystanders. At the same time he relished the admiration and appreciation of men of the world and of scientists. He was delighted to have brought a smile to the face of the Queen who was notorious for not being amused. Her Majesty's normally impassive face was wreathed in smiles when the missionary told her that Africans who wanted to know about the White Queen's wealth, always inquired how many royal cows she possessed.

As to his broken romance, it comes as a great surprise to learn that he was more than ordinarily interested in Catherine Ridley. What one would have gathered was his usual, unromantic attitude is bluntly expressed in a reply to a routine question in a questionnaire from the L.M.S. on his marital status. ' Under no obligation as to a marriage; never made proposals of marriage; nor so conducted myself to any woman to cause her to suspect that I intended anything related to marriage.' These are the words of a misogynist! But it was only after he reached London that he became vulnerable. The existence of this romance came to light recently when there came into the possession of the Trustees of the Livingstone Memorial at Blantyre a copy of Sigourney's *Lays of the West*, a missionary volume, with the inscription in Livingstone's hand, ' To Cathrine [spelt so!] Ridley with the best wishes and Christian regards of D.L. London. 25th June 1840.' It seems that she, two brothers named Prentice (one of whom she later married) and Livingstone formed part of a group of young missionary enthusiasts in Chipping Ongar where Livingstone was directed to spend six months in theological studies. He was impressed by her charm and education. Her name, hitherto unidentifiable, often recurs in the letters he sent to his London friends during his first few years in Africa. When he left for Africa she presented him with two keepsakes, a watchguard and a devotional volume which he perused on the voyage ' with heavenly-minded reflections '. She did not come out to Africa, probably for health reasons, and there is no evidence that she met Livingstone afterwards.

This wound to Livingstone's heart was superficial, but the defection of his eldest son Robert drove a deep gash into the missionary's heart. The father felt that Robert's life was a disgrace, but by modern standards it was nothing more than wilful insubordination. He had, as might be expected in a son of such a father, a determined will of of his own, which developed all the more strongly in the absence of parental control. As an adolescent he was sent out to his father in South Africa, but, finding it impossible to be conveyed up country from Natal, he returned to Liverpool, and nothing was heard of him thereafter. The disappearance of this son of a man of public eminence was naturally the subject of much tittle-tattle, distasteful to the father. Of his later life little is known, except that he enlisted in the Northern Army during the American Civil War under the roystering pseudonym of 'Rupert Vincent' and was wounded at the battle of Laurel Hill, Virginia, and died of wounds in the Salisbury prison-camp, at the age of eighteen. Livingstone reproached himself bitterly for not having spent more time with his children, when he unveiled his heart to Stanley in Ujiji. He found some consolation, however, in the thought that his son gave his life, as he did his own, for the healing of the 'Open Sore of Africa' — slavery.

Earlier, we asked whether Livingstone was aesthetically a Philistine, utterly insensitive to art and music. In reply, it may be said that few have been aware of the healing beauties of Nature as he was, and that he accounted religion and the contemplation of natural beauty the two defence-mechanisms against the degeneration inevitable in living for years amongst a primitive and heathen population. He was not otherwise interested in art (for his water-colours are accurate rather than inspired recordings). His perpetual singing of hymn-tunes irritated his Zambezi colleague, Kirk, probably because they were sung out of tune. The latter reported: 'When the weather gets foul or anything goes wrong it is well to give him a wide berth, especially when he sings to himself. But the air is some indication. If it is the "Happy Land" then look out for squalls and stand clear! If "Scots wha hae" there is some grand vision before his mind.'

Our conclusion must recount something of his inner and devotional life. If must not be forgotten that he was first and foremost a missionary, exploration being a secondary consideration and strictly subordinate to his path-breaking for the Gospel. He had the highest conception of the missionary's task, as recorded in his famous words: 'God had only one Son and He was a missionary.' In his own judgment he was not less a missionary when searching for trade-routes from Central Africa to the coast which would, by opening up the way to honest commerce, tend to smother the nefarious commerce of trading in human lives which had appealed to the cupidity of African chiefs for European goods. ' Neither civilization nor Christianity ', he wrote, ' can be promoted alone. In fact, they are inseparable.'

A man's real faith emerges (or is submerged, if feeble) in hardship and loneliness. Livingstone's invincible faith shines brightest through the darkness of the *Last Journals*. He was a Calvinist, but not an unlovely one. The great strength of his life came from his assurance both of the sovereignty of God and of his own election as an instrument of God. Had he been less reticent by nature, he would have adopted Coillard's *credo* as expressing his own deepest thoughts: ' I am immortal until my work is done.' His daily dependence upon God and his continual companionship with Christ were the steel of his soul, the secret source of his dynamic personality.

This companionship was fed by the regular nourishment of the Bible, for him the living Word of God. When he had a forced wait of several months until new carriers should reach him on his last journey into the interior, he wrote in his Journal (entry of 3 Oct. 1871): ' I read the whole Bible through four times while I was at Manyuema.' The pocket Testament which he carried with him (now preserved at the Blantyre Memorial) indicates that, apart from the Gospels, his favourite reading was in the Psalms. His iron-ration consisted of the 40th to the 43rd Psalms inclusive, the 90th, 95th, the 113th, and especially the 23rd and the 121st. These are most heavily thumb-marked.

The dedication of his life is summed up felicitously in the prayer included in his Journal in the entry for 19 March of the last year of his life: ' My birthday. My Jesus, my King, my Life, my All, I again dedicate my whole self to Thee. Accept me and grant, O gracious Father, that ere this year is gone I may finish my work. In Jesu's name I ask it. Amen.'

The quiet confidence of his faith enabled him to face the threatenings of men and of Nature unafraid. It is supremely important to remember that when he died at Ilala on 1 May 1873, his African comrades found him in a kneeling posture beside his bed. It was characteristic of him that, although emaciated and terribly weakened by fever, his last effort was the expression of his love for God.

The same love for God was expressed in his lifelong service of men. This was reciprocated in the magnificent tribute of his African colleagues who bore his body through 1,500 difficult miles on a nine months journey from Ilala to Bagamayo, a few miles from the East Coast. No other single event has so impressed the world with the deep potentialities of the African character. Livingstone's greatest distinction was his discovery, not of the African hinterland, but of the hinterland of the African personality. The universal brotherhood that he practised was disclosed in the spirit and the example of Jesus Christ whose servant he was.

CHAPTER X

FRANCIS PFANNER

TO-DAY Mariannhill in Natal is a vast Roman Catholic community, complete with monastery and convent, pro-cathedral, workshops, hospitals, training college, practising school and industrial school. Seventy years ago it was little more than a thought in the devout mind of its founder, Father Francis Pfanner, who reached South Africa in 1880. The vision of the founder, admirably seconded by the religious and secular members of the Trappist Order, has been amply repaid in the astonishing harvest of 140,000 souls which it is claimed to have reaped. The trainees of the order, religious and lay, are to be found in churches, schools and workshops, from Umtata to Bulawayo and beyond.

So wide a harvest argues a remarkable ploughman of the Spirit. Such in fact, Father Pfanner was. He was a twin born to farming parents at Langen in the lovely Austrian Tyrol in 1825, who was christened Wendolin. As a schoolboy he might have been described as an intense all-rounder, rather than a brilliant student or athlete. His favourite recreation was wrestling, and it is not too fanciful to regard the main task of his life as wrestling with God for the souls of men. Red-haired men make admirable fighters, whether they wrestle with ' flesh and blood ' or with ' principalities and powers '. He was normal enough to flame up at the taunt ' Carrots '!

His first University was Innsbrück, where he studied philosophy with acumen, and managed to irritate the pedants by his boisterousness. From Innsbrück he crossed the Alps for a further year of study at the famous Italian

University of Padua. Here, however, he and his companions were not very happy. They seem to have forsaken their first love of philosophy, because, in their haste to shake the dust of the city off their feet (aided by a physician's certificate of ill-health), ' we remembered to say good-bye only to our beloved old Professor of Physics '. The other explanation may be that this venerable gentleman was a fellow-countryman of theirs.

In 1846 Wendolin became convinced that his vocation was to be the priesthood and in the autumn of this year he began theological studies in the Seminary of Brixen in Austria. His mind was bent on missionary work. ' As often as I recited the verse in the *Miserere* (prescribed in our rule for daily recitation), " I will teach the unjust Thy ways, and the wicked shall be converted to Thee ", the yearning and desire to work in the badly neglected missions tormented me and gave me no rest ', he writes in his Memoirs. His episcopal adviser dissuaded him temporarily from missionary work because he was physically a weakling! He completed his seminary studies in 1850 and in the same year was ordained to the priesthood.

From the beginning of his ministry for God he refused to take insults seriously. His first parish, Haselstauden, where he was appointed administrator, was rent with dissensions and it is therefore not surprising that not one member of his Church in this thickly-populated village offered either to greet him or help him to unload the furniture. What is surprising, is that he refused to be hurt by this deliberate insult. After three years as acting-vicar of the parish, he had so won the affection and admiration of his parishioners that they elected him as their pastor by ballot. There he remained for nine years, and might have remained for ever, had not an unsought opportunity for special service come his way. It appears that the Austrian Sisters of Charity, working in Jugoslavia, had lost their chaplain, and that the Bishop of

Brixen recommended Father Pfanner to take his place.
He was spiritual director to over a hundred nuns, and
while appreciating the privilege of his office, found it in
time rather monotonous.

In 1862 he left the convent of Agram for a visit to the
Eternal City. He was uncertain as to what form his
future work should take, when he met two Belgian Trappist monks, and was fascinated by their account of the
type of religious life they lived. With the approval of
his Bishop, his application to join the Trappist Monastery
of Maria Wald (Marywood) was accepted.

His decision is explained by a letter he wrote about this
time to his people at home: ' I realize that monastic life
will require courage and sacrifice. I beg of you to pray
for me that I may have the strength to comply with all
that shall be demanded of me. As for myself, I shall not
miss physical comforts, riches or honours. I seek nothing
in the world but to live poor and unknown in the service
of my God.'

It was the renunciation of the Trappist Order that his
ebullient spirit seemed most to need. The Reformed
Cistercians (the official name for the Trappist Order) are
renowned for their austerities, which consist of taking one
vegetarian meal each day, and abstaining from literature
and speech, except under specially urgent circumstances.
At the age of thirty-eight Wendolin was invested and
received the alternative name of Francis. For three years
he filled various offices in the monastery, until in 1867
he received an important commission — to found a new
monastery of the order. After overcoming almost endless
difficulties, he and his seven assistants purchased a site near
Banjaluka in Jugoslavia. The first monastery of Maria
Stern (Mary the Star) was merely a fifteen-foot long
barn, with apertures in the boards large enough to allow
the sparrows to join the monks at their frugal meals. A
small number could live in such austerity, but the number

of novices, increasing the community to sixty, made a new building imperative. This, too, was erected only with great difficulties for the sixty-roomed building was thought by the Turkish Pasha of the neighbourhood to be a fortress. It was, of course, but not a military fortress, and all Father Francis's astuteness was necessary to allay the acute suspicions of the Mohammedan official. In 1879, Father Francis was recalled to the Mother House to be informed that Maria Stern was to be raised to the status of an Abbey, and that he was to be its first Abbot.

The next day was to bring a startling reversal in the direction of his life. At a general meeting of the Chapter of the Abbots and Priors of the Trappist Order in Sept-Fons, France, Bishop Ricards of Grahamstown made an impassioned appeal for volunteers for missionary work in South Africa. It was met with a frozen silence, broken only by the quiet words, ' If no one will go, I will '. To everyone's amazement the voice was that of the Abbot-elect of Maria Stern, then fifty-four years of age. Remembering the toil of his life, and the expectation of peace in his Jugoslavian monastery, soon to be an abbey, who can doubt the heroism that inspired the answer?

He returned for a few weeks to Maria Stern in order to leave the administration in good order and bid farewell to his colleagues. On 28 July 1880 he and his co-volunteers set foot on South African soil at Port Elizabeth. Their cross-country journey brought then to Dunbrody, and they took up residence in a shanty overgrown with brambles and set in a chaos of cacti. For nine months they fought to clear the bush and to cultivate the arid, drought-stricken land. So impossible was the situation that Father Francis had to leave for Europe to consult with the Superiors of the Order. While overseas, he learned that Bishop Jolivet of Natal was anxious for the Trappists to settle in Natal. The community in Dunbrody was ordered to leave for Natal, which they did late in 1882. By December of this year they had purchased land some fifteen miles from Durban and three from Pinetown, which is to-day part of the site of Mariannhill. It was given the latter name by the founder as a dedication to the Blessed Virgin and to her mother Saint Anne.

At the end of the first year Mariannhill was able to boast a chapel, a chapter-room, a refectory, dormitory, bakery, workshops for tinsmiths, blacksmiths, wagon-makers and printers, a photographic studio, a school for Africans and residential facilities attached, in addition to a guest-house, stables, and miniature farm. Roads were built and dams were constructed, in a remarkably short time. But these were all means to the spiritual end. The first fruits of the spiritual work came in 1884 when four African boys were baptized.

The next year the monastery was raised to the status of an abbey and Prior Francis became for the second time in his life, Abbot Pfanner. In the same year a special Sisters' Congregation, the Sisters of the Precious Blood, was established in order to teach African girls, but it has since developed into an independent missionary congregation with branches all over the world. The Abbot was the inspirational centre of a vast missionary, educational and social enterprise radiating from Mariannhill. New mission stations were set up, the first at Reichenau on the Polela River, 130 miles away; the second at Einsiedeln, 40 miles from Mariannhill. The momentum of Mariannhill seems to have been irresistible, until to-day there are almost 300 churches in three Vicariates at Mariannhill, Umtata, and Bulawayo.

The wisdom of the founder was seen in his wide interpretation of the implications of the Gospel, to include not only better souls, but better homes, better fields, better social conditions, as preparations for better hearts! Yet it was this very interpretation which was to gain for him

the disapproval of the Superiors of the Order which tech-
nically is not a missionary order. To the numbed amazement of the Mariannhill fathers he was summarily sus-
pended from office in 1892. The former Abbot now
retired to the mission station he had founded, Lourdes,
and, with great self-abnegation, did not choose to return
to Mariannhill when the year of enforced isolation was
over, lest he should alienate the loyalties of the fathers
from his successor. He was perhaps greatest in the charity
and submissiveness of spirit with which he met this the
heaviest blow to his hopes. In April 1894, he left for a
remote place in the Skimper's Nek mountains, where he
meant to spend the rest of his life. With characteristic
hope he named it *Emmaus*, and he came to believe that he
was more deeply united with His crucified Lord in these
years of suffering than ever before. For eleven years
here he rose at 3.0 a.m. for devotions and preparation for
the Mass, breakfasting five hours later. Most of the
morning was spent in manual labour of the roughest kind.
The rest of the day was spent in prayer, meditation,
reading, and a walk of an hour, and, after a final recitation
of the Office, he retired at eight in the evening. Even
when rheumatoid arthritis afflicted him, he was insistent
upon rising by 4.0 a.m. to make his Communion. He died
in 1909 at eighty-four years of age.

The tension between the missionary obligations of
Mariannhill and the strict monastic rule of the Trappist
Order was finally resolved four years after the founder's
death by the Pope, Pius X. The Mariannhill missionary
fathers and brothers were separated from the Trappist
Order and made an entirely distinct missionary congregation. This meant that they had their own rule of life,
distinct constitution and distinctive habit.

Thus the challenge accepted by a fifty-four-year-old
Austrian monk in France led to the missionary expansion
of Roman Catholicism in South Africa, and thence to the

erection of daughter-houses, schools and social work in countries as distant as Holland, England, Switzerland, Poland, Canada and the U.S.A. In such a vision of the Church transcending national and racial frontiers, and redeeming the environment as well as the souls of youth and adults, lies the invincible hope of Mariannhill for the future. And the realization of that vision owes most, under God, to Francis Pfanner, the founder.

CHAPTER XI

ANDREW MURRAY

HIS old friend, Professor J. I. Marais, summed up Andrew Murray's significance in the words: ' He is essentially a man of prayer and at the same time a man of affairs.' His admirable biographer, Prof. J. du Plessis, goes so far as to claim that he combined the qualities of John Wesley and William Law. Certainly his congregations in Bloemfontein, Worcester, Cape Town and Wellington knew that his sermons were prepared on his knees; but a wider world gleaned the literary fruits of his meditation. For he wrote 240 books and pamphlets, many of which have appeared in fifteen different languages in translation. He was South Africa's greatest devotional writer, and the reading of his classic *Abide in Christ* is reported to have started a Christian revival in China! Such was the cosmic spiritual influence generated by this truly South African minister in whose veins flowed both Dutch and Scottish blood.

As a man of affairs his influence was not less, whether as educationalist, missionary statesman, or churchman. Of whom else could it be said that he had founded two university colleges, a normal college, and a missionary training institute, mainly on his own initiative? As churchman he had won in a unique degree the confidence of the Cape Synod of the Dutch Reformed Church, which elected him to the Moderatorship, the supreme office in the Church, no less than six times. The wonder is, with all these responsibilities, that Murray's compassion, humility and patience were untarnished, and that he remained the most lovable character in nineteenth-century South Africa!

Andrew Murray was born a son of the manse. His father (whose Christian name he bore) came out from Scotland to Cape Town in 1822 on the recommendation of the Rev. Dr. George Thom and became the sixth minister of the Dutch Reformed congregation at Graaff-Reinet, where he ministered for forty-five years. Andrew Murray, junior, was born in the dignified Parsonage on 9 May 1828, almost two years after his brother and companion, John. This splendid house (which still stands) was his home for the first seven years of his life, and he played in its flower and fruit gardens, and often walked or ran down the avenue of orange-trees alternating with lilac-trees to the plot of lucerne for the cow and the field of oats for the horses. Here his ten brothers and sisters were born. His mother, Maria Susanna Stegman, was of Huguenot and Lutheran ancestry, and she was as gracious a Christian as his father. Andrew and John were the firmest of friends, and no one was more delighted than Andrew when his brilliant brother became a foundation professor of Stellenbosch's famous Theological Seminary. It was a large and happy family, and in the life of South Africa it was to wield an influence proportionate to its size. That was considerable, for Andrew and Maria Susanna Murray had ninety-one grandchildren!

Education in the country districts of the Cape was most inadequate in those early days, for it was mainly provided by discharged soldiers who tramped from farm to farm to give their tuition. Their father determined to send the two boys to Aberdeen in Scotland where their uncle, Dr. John Murray, held an important pastorate. Andrew and John joined the ship at Port Elizabeth, and their foster-father for the journey was the renowned Wesleyan missionary, the Rev. James Archbell, then proceding home on leave. The very next day after the boys reached Aberdeen, their diligent uncle entered them as pupils of the city's Grammar School. During their seven years' stay in

Scotland an ecclesiastical dispute was raging between those who favoured and those who abhorred the state establishment of the Presbyterian Church. Their uncle was one of the leaders of the Free Church party.

The boys worked well at school, anxious to prove that young South Africans were as able and industrious as their Scots companions. Nevertheless, despite their later success at university they were not outstanding at school. This is made clear in an amusing anti-climax contained in one of Andrew's letters home: ' We delayed answering it (their father's letter) till we should see what our success should be at the end of the session. That success, however, has been very small: John has gotten the seventh prize in Mathematics.' At Aberdeen University, however, they were distinguished students. In 1845 (when Andrew was not quite seventeen) both brothers graduated as Masters of Arts, after an examination, lasting seven days, in: the Evidences of Christianity, Latin, Greek, Natural History, Moral Philosophy, Natural Philosophy, Mathematics and Logic. John Murray obtained his M.A. with distinction.

The next three years the brothers spent at Utrecht University. By now they had decided on the Christian ministry as their calling and their father wanted them to study at the famous Dutch university to complete their theological training, to learn Dutch (the right medium for a ministry in the Dutch Reformed Church) and to prepare for ordination at the hands of the Hague Commission. Their father was, none the less, fearful of the dangers of university life and warned them:

> Allow me to say that I liked Holland very much indeed. At first, being what the people called an *Engelschman*, they overcharged me. . . . One temptation you will be exposed to through companionship is the use of Hollands [i.e. gin] and water and smoking tobacco or cigars. Resist both these abominable customs.

7

After seven years' absence from the Cape, their Dutch had became rusty, and the brothers had to address staff and students in Latin, the academic Esperanto of the day. At this time, the acids of Rationalism were corroding the fabric of the orthodox Christian faith in Holland, but the brothers were alive to the danger. They joined the student society *Sechor Dabar* (Remember the Word), which was founded to combat heresy. This society, like the ' Holy Club ' of Oxford associated with the Wesleys, consisted of Christians pledged to the discipline of the spiritual life and to philanthropic endeavours. The Murrays also had the distinction of founding *Eltheto*, a society to promote interest in missions among undergraduates which survived until the present century, when it was incorporated into the Netherlands Student Christian Association. In their experience and training they were well equipped to fight the twin dangers of Erastianism (State control) and Scepticism, when they should raise their ugly heads in the Cape. On 9 May 1848 they were ordained.

In November they returned to the Cape, and Andrew preached his first sermon in the Groote Kerk in the Heerengracht (now Adderley Street) of Cape Town. Ecclesiastical preferment was in the hands of the Governor, Sir Harry Smith. He sent John, the elder brother, to the more eligible charge of Burghersdorp, and to Andrew he said: ' As you are the younger, I am afraid I shall have to send you to Bloemfontein.'

As it transpired, this was a more suitable charge for a young man of Andrew's mettle, and here he was to be the spiritual leader of a vast territory beyond the Orange River, with an area of 50,000 square miles. Three days after his twenty-first birthday he celebrated his induction. His influence among the sturdy farmers and hard-headed business men of British and Dutch extraction was much greater than his years. Here he was incessantly preaching, planning and journeying. He went to the Wittebergen

(Bethlehem), or to the Natal border (Harrismith), or up to the Mooi River (now Potchefstroom), where the Trekking Boers took exception to the state-appointed predikants of the Dutch Reformed Church. Murray's genial and sincere personality overcame their suspicions and gained him a welcome from Andries Pretorius. Indeed, they were most anxious to obtain his services as their permanent minister in the neighbourhood of Potchefstroom. Apart from his work in Bloemfontein, Murray was consulent (or, acting minister) at Riet River, Rietpoort and Winburg.

He was superbly fitted, by his bilingualism and reconciling nature, to be a mediator between the British Government and the Transvaal. In fact, he acted as translator at the Sand River Convention of 1852, which was intended to guarantee the independence of the Transvaal.

A fascinating and unsolicited testimonial to the forthrightness of his preaching was given by a Transvaal African, and recorded by the Rev. J. H. Neethling. The Native said:

> I never thought that the white men stood in such fear of their chiefs. Look at the young chief yonder [i.e. Murray]. He points his finger at the people: they sit quiet. He threatens them: they sit quite still. He storms and rages at them: they sit as quiet as death.

Murray's integrity and impartiality were again in demand in 1853, when a National Convention was held in Bloemfontein, which nominated Dr. Frazer and himself as delegates to go to England to dissuade the British Government from abandoning the Orange River Sovereignty. The delegates had an interview with the Duke of Newcastle (Secretary of State for the Colonies), but it was three weeks after the Convention of Bloemfontein was ratified, ceding power to J. P. Hoffman and his colleagues who agreed to form their own administration of the Orange Free State. While in London, Murray was invited to take temporary charge of the influential Surrey Chapel in the metropolis. He declined, but was exhilarated in the experience of preaching to a congregation of 3,000 souls.

He was also commissioned by the Cape Synod to seek out ministers for the Colony in Scotland and Holland. The difficulties made him an ardent advocate for the establishment of a Theological Seminary in the Cape to train an indigenous ministry. This ideal was realized on 3 November 1857, in the foundation of Stellenbosch Theological Seminary.

The year 1856 was important in his Bloemfontein ministry. He was then married to Emma Rutherfoord, the daughter of a worthy Cape Town merchant, who was the foundation treasurer of the 'Cape of Good Hope Society for aiding deserving Slaves and Slave-children to purchase their Freedom'. Mr. Rutherfoord was returned a year later as the member representing the Western Province in the House of Assembly. The year 1856 was also important in that Murray was elected one of the three foundation Trustees of Grey College, Bloemfontein. He became Rector of this institution, and his co-operative wife took many boarders in their home. Thus Murray was a founder of the future University College of the Orange Free State, which has recently attained the status of an independent university.

In 1860 Murray received and accepted a call to the Church of Worcester. His ministry here was marked by an astonishing spiritual revival, which swept fifty men into the ranks of the ministry, and hundreds into the membership of the Church. Here also he wrote, in 1864, his great devotional classic, *Blijf in Jezus* (translated as *Abide in Christ*), which he prepared as a manual in Christian discipleship for the many new converts of the Revival. This was Murray's attempt to counter the emotionalism of the Revival. In 1862, at the age of thirty-four, he was elected Moderator at the Quinquennial Synod of the Cape. At this historic Synod Murray led the struggle against Rationalism and Erastianism, which threatened to disrupt the life of the Church. His Liberal opponents included the Revs. J. J. Kotze of Darling and T. F. Burgers (who later became President of the Transvaal). Although the majority of ministers wished to depose these able but unorthodox men, their judgment was not upheld by the Civil Courts. Andrew Murray himself defended the action of the Synod. When he ended his speech of four and a half hours, he was complimented by Mr. Justice Bell in these words: 'Few advocates could have done it equally well.'

He was called to the most influential pulpit in the entire Church in 1864, that of Cape Town's Groote Kerk, as colleague of the venerable Dr. Heyns and Dr. Abraham Faure. On his younger shoulders fell the main weight of this exacting charge, in which the communicant members numbered 3,000 and the adherents 5,000. He still managed to make time for outside interests, becoming the first President of the Cape Town Y.M.C.A. in 1865. What respite he would allow himself from his duties was spent in the delightful *pastorie* in Kloof Street on the slopes of Lion's Head, with its outlook on to Table Bay. On their flower-girdled lawns the Murrays played one of the earliest games of croquet in the Cape. In those days Mrs. Murray's sewing-machine was an equally rare sight.

Andrew Murray will always be associated with Wellington. In 1871 he went there to commence a ministry that lasted thirty-four years. Here his missionary zeal found its fullest outlet, for he taught his Church members to be missionaries to the Coloured people; and here in 1877 he founded the famous Wellington Missionary Training Institute. Here, too, he established the renowned Huguenot Seminary in 1874. It was to be a training college for intending teachers and an institution of higher education for other women. Its distinctive ethos was the Christian spirit, and it had a unique domestic arrangement by which household tasks were to be performed by the students themselves for their own good, and also to keep the fees low enough for girls of modest means to gain admittance. The ideals of the Seminary were based on the work of Mary Lyon, the founder of Mount Holyoke College in Massachusetts. It has, of course, since become known throughout South Africa as the Huguenot University College,* the only university institution founded in South Africa for women.

Murray, as we have seen, was a keen educationalist. As co-founder of Bloemfontein's Grey College, and of the Normal College in Cape Town, as sole founder of the Huguenot Seminary (with its two daughter seminaries) and the Missionary Training Institute in Wellington, he has no equal. It was entirely fitting that he should be honoured with the Doctorate of Divinity of his old University of Aberdeen in 1898, and by the Doctorate of Literature of the University of the Cape of Good Hope in 1907.

He has many other claims to South Africa's appreciation: as author, as missionary statesman, as patriotic friend of Europeans of both British and Dutch extraction, as the father of a family that has rendered unparalleled service in Church, school, and mission field. His greatest claim to fame lies in his own spiritual force. He was in the succession of the saints, and all tributes to him indicate that he was characterized by a deep earnestness of faith, an absolute dedication to his calling, and a lofty nobility of character. Few men surely have accomplished so much

---

* Huguenot University College ceased to exist as a University institution on 31 December 1950. The College buildings, much of its equipment, and its endowments were taken over by the *Armesorg Kommissie* of the Dutch Reformed Church to be used for the training of Mission Social Workers. The new institution is to be known as the Huguenot College.

for the Master, and yet remained so humble. One incident illuminates this grace in him. A young probationer who was invited to become his assistant replied impertinently that he feared he would be unable to agree with Dr. Murray in everything. Unruffled, the venerable pastor replied: ' Come! In everything in which you cannot agree with me, I will agree with you.' It was significant that his long and gracious life came to an end, in 1917, as he had lived — in prayer.

A world immersed in getting and spending looks with amazement at the sheer other-worldliness and holiness of Andrew Murray. No man gazed more steadily at the golden towers and citadels of eternity through the mists of time. Men, so compassionate and incorruptible, are the nation's most precious assets.

We may close with a tribute paid by the late Hon. John X. Merriman, Prime Minister of the Cape:

> If ever there was a dweller in the household of faith it was Andrew Murray. . . . It was given to him, a Calvinist, to write books of devotion that met with the highest commendation at the hands of the most High Church Anglican bishops — books which have been a source of consolation and comfort to many weary souls in travail in many lands and of many creeds. . . . Well for us all would it be if we could bury in his grave that racial bitterness and social discord against which his whole life was a protest.

CHAPTER XII

KHAMA BOIKANO

THE spotlight of world publicity has played on Seretse Khama, claimant to the chieftainship of the Bamangwato, one of the leading tribes of the Bechuana people; but it is not widely known that only thirty years ago the chief of the Bamangwato was also in the world headlines. This man's name was Khama Boikano and he was renowned as 'Khama the Good'. In England he was the most successful missionary deputation that the London Missionary Society ever had, for he was that rare phenomenon, a Christian African ruler. He is included in this series as a refutation of the barbarous assertion that the African must for ever remain uncivilized and heathen. He was neither. His distinction as a Christian is all the greater when it is recognized that in making his decision he had to fight the immemorial traditions of his tribe and that his mental pilgrimage from heathenism to Christianity represents as long and dramatic a journey as the proverbial success story of 'From log-cabin to White House'. For him, moreover, Christianity was no mere gloss or patina but a deep and constant conviction. No gallery of Great Christians in South Africa would be complete which excluded so distinguished a Christian Bantu. The missionary who had spent most of his years in Khama's 'Great Place', the Rev. J. D. Hepburn, writes of him:

I know no other Interior Chief who has even *attempted* the half that Khama has accomplished in the advancing of his people towards the goal of civilization.

The missionary's wife pays as great a tribute to his Christianity as her husband did to his encouragement of civilization:

For months at a time while my husband was visiting the Lake Ngami people, have I been left with my children under Khama's sole protection and guardianship; and no brother could have cared for us more thoughtfully and kindly. . . . In all our intercourse I can most gratefully say that he was to me always a true Christian gentleman in word and deed. No one now living knows 'Khama the Good' as I know him. Did they do so, they could but honour and trust him, as I do from my heart.

Chief Khama is a vindication both of the great potentialities of the African character, and of the transforming power of the Christian Gospel. Sceptics may well ponder the words directed against them by James Russell Lowell:

. . . these men living in ease and luxury, indulging themselves in the amusement of going without a religion, may be thankful that they live in lands where the gospel they neglect has tamed the beastliness and ferocity of the men who, but for Christianity, might long ago have eaten their carcasses like the South Sea Islanders, or cut off their heads and tanned their hides, like the monsters of the French Revolution.

The same point of view was expressed more racily by an American airman who made a forced landing in New Guinea, and wrote home:

Dear Mom. Thanks to Missions, I was feasted and not feasted upon when I fell from the sky into this village.

This incident is a citation from a letter given in Henry P. Van Dusen's book *They Found the Church There*. With equal justification it could be plausibly argued that but for the reconciling influence of missions South Africa might still be engaged in a series of Kaffir Wars. Chief Khama is then a triumph of the Christian Gospel and a vindication of the success of missionaries. Khama stands out against the background of his tribal history as a Christian gentleman among unmitigated, if bold and sagacious, savages. Son of a crafty, treacherous and cruel sorcerer, with the blood of generations of paganism in his veins, he ruled the

Bamangwato people for fifty years with unwavering justice, high courage — and here is the miracle — with Christian standards.

His tribe, the Bamangwato ('children of Ngwato'), will explain the meaning of their name as 'a poor piece of beef'. Tradition says that this was the gift made to Ngwato's mother by her sarcastic husband when she seemed sterile. When, however, she bore him the coveted son and heir, she named him Ngwato (or, 'Contempt') as a reminder to her boorish husband. The tribal totem is the duiker. It is significant that Khama's father venerated the totem and would never step over a mat of duiker skins; Khama, by contrast, openly ate duiker steaks to show his emancipation from the ancient taboo.

Sekhome, Khama's father and the chief, was a renowned sorcerer. Cunning, alert, fearless, energetic and wise, he was a man to be feared. John Mackenzie, J. D. Hepburn's predecessor as L.M.S. missionary in Bechuanaland, declared that he kept twelve wives and the children of these unions were many, but the most important of them all was Khama, the elder son by his chief wife.

Khama was born in 1830* and lived to be a nonagenarian. His birth is dated from the fact that it took place shortly after the terrifying days when Mzilikazi's Matebele warriors made their historic exodus from Natal to the neighbourhood of the present Bulawayo in 1827. The Bamangwato women fled to the security of the flats and on their return in 1830 Khama Boikwano was born to Keamogetze, Sekhome's first wife. She lived until 1875, when Khama took over the chieftainship.

By all the laws of eugenics he should have been a supersavage, a scheming black butcher in a red blanket, destined to lead his tribe to oblivion through its decimation

* Khama may, according to Dr. Edwin Smith, have been born in 1835, for a Baptismal Register of 1860 gives his age as 25.

and destruction by war, famine, pestilence and ' Cape-smoke '.   Lord Lugard has stated that Bantu chiefs often took their wives from north-west and north-east African stock which had reached a higher stage of civilization than their southernmost kinsmen, and he goes on to suggest that Khama may have come from such stock.   Khama's own answer would have been that the entail of superstition was broken by the transforming grace of God.

Khama first heard Christian teaching from the lips of Livingstone and Moffat, but he was baptized by the Rev. Mr. Schulenburg of the Hermannsburg mission in 1858. The latter Society, through lack of financial support, had to withdraw from Bechuanaland, and the task of training the chief's sons as Christians was handed on to the mission-aries of the London Society including Roger Price, John Mackenzie and J. D. Hepburn.   In his early years Khama became a courageous Christian, despite his father's pro-tests of unpatriotism.   This is known from the words that Sekhome said to Mackenzie: ' It is all very good for you white people to follow the Word of God; God made you with straight hearts, but it is a very different thing with us black people; God made us with crooked hearts. Mackenzie replied, ' Nay, Sekhome, those who turn to God get a new heart and better thoughts.'   ' Not black people ', retorted Sekhome, ' and yet, and yet after all, Khama's heart is perhaps white.   Yet, Khama's heart is white.'

Khama soon had an opportunity to prove that Christian-ity had not shorn him of his valour.   In 1863 a messenger rushed into Sekhome's camp to inform him that the Mate-bele army was already on its way to attack the Bamang-wato.   Sekhome prepared for war both as commander-in-chief and as chief witch-doctor, throwing his bones and muttering potent incarnations.   Khama interrupted, saying he was uninterested in this superstitious mumbo-jumbo, and that he wanted to settle the menace by fighting.   The chief then ordered out the two youngest regiments under

Khama and his brother Khamane. Two hundred men moved off to do battle with a vastly superior force. Though outnumbered and outmanoeuvred, Khama's men valiantly attacked the Matebele and killed three of the five sons of Mzilikazi. One of the two survivors, Lobengula (afterwards the scourge of the Mashona and Batawana tribes), received a bullet in the neck that had been fired by Khama and which he carried to the day of his death. The foemen threatened to return, but because of respect for Khama they desisted. Mzilikazi and Lobengula declared: ' The Bamangwato are dogs; Khama is a man!' Thus Khama won his spurs as a warrior.

He was equally renowned as an intrepid hunter. On one occasion he went with a large party to hunt a lion which had killed many cattle. Several hunters had tried to kill the beast, but all had failed. Each night round the campfire the men boasted what they would do on the following day when they encountered the beast. Khama was silent. But one morning, as dawn was breaking, some of them awoke to find a man approaching with the skin of a large lion thrown carelessly over his shoulder. It was Khama — he had despatched the lion single-handed while they slept.

Khama's continual task was to prove his loyalty to the tribe, while dissenting from its heathen customs. An open break with the tribe took place in 1865 when the ceremony of *boguera* or circumcision was to be held. This initiation to manhood and the customs of the tribe was obligatory on all the males of the tribe. Because of Khama's refusal to participate, Sekhome threw all his authority and influence against the missionaries and the African Christians. Khama and Khamane waged a kind of Christian resistance movement in the tribe, greatly to their own jeopardy.

Another issue which brought them into conflict with the tribal practice was marriage. The two Christian brothers had married the daughters of Chikudu, a leading headman of the tribe, which roused the jealousy of the other headmen. Sekhome tried to force Khama to displace his wife by urging that he must go through with an arrangement made years before to marry the daughter of Pelutona, a famous sorcerer and rain-maker. Sekhome's aim was twofold: first, to make Pelutona's daughter Khama's primary wife and displace his present wife, and second, to bring Khama under the influence of the sorcerer. Khama's response was: 'I refuse on account of the Word of God to take a second wife.' Because of this defiance, Sekhome ordered his men to fire the huts of his two intractable sons. To his consternation they absolutely refused. Now, by all the tribal laws to which he had appealed, his own life should have been forfeit to his sons. So he fled, expecting a counterplot to terminate his life. To his amazement Khama's messenger sent to ask him to return as chief, on condition that he did not persecute the Christians or persist in requesting Khama's re-marriage.

It looked as though Khama's Christian forgiveness was wasted on Sekhome, for once a plotter always a plotter. He now intrigued to recall Macheng, his brother, the lawful chief, under cover of whose weak rule he would plan to murder Khama and Khamane, then remove Macheng, and thus rule without a rival. When the unsuspecting Macheng arrived to assume the chieftainship of the tribe, Khama's was the only discordant note among the flattering speeches with which he was welcomed. Khama declared, with an honesty unusual on such occasions:

I say I am not glad to see you. If Sekhome could not live with his own children but drove them from the town and shot at them, how is he to submit to be ruled by you?... There are two Chiefs already, and I refuse to be called the third, as some of you have mockingly named me. My kingdom henceforth consists of my horses, my rifle and my wagon.

Khama, learning of a plot to assassinate Macheng, informed him of Sekhome's treachery and they made common cause against him.   Next it was Macheng's turn to
prove the villain, but the failure of his attempt to poison
Khama, and his consequent unpopularity, left Khama with
a clear field.   In 1875 he became chief of the Bamangwato,
by the unanimous election of the headmen.

He was to continue a faithful Christian in days of prosperity, as he had been in days of adversity.   Indeed, such
was his enthusiasm for the faith that he maintained the
work of the Church and the day-school during the three
years that Mackenzie, the missionary, was in England on
furlough.

As chief, Khama was to discover that there is a strife
of God, as well as a peace of God.   He set himself to the
task of eradicating superstition and civilizing the tribe.
As a Christian ruler he had three problems to face. Firstly,
there was the question of heathen ceremonies, which were
the warp and woof of the social life of the people.   When
the season arrived for the communal planting of the
gardens, Khama called the tribe together, told them that
he disliked but would not prohibit heathen ceremonies,
but they must not be performed in the *kgotla* or public
courtyard.   Then proving that he wished to fulfil, not
destroy, he invited Mackenzie to conduct a Christian
service.

His second problem was the moral damage caused by
the selling of strong drink to the Natives by white men.
The chief drink imported was brandy, fortified by tobacco
juice and other more insidious ingredients.   It was a source
of profit to the sellers and of degradation to the consumers.
Khama declared it illegal to sell strong drink in the town
or to bring it into the country.   The next weekend several
of the white men were hopelessly drunk.   Khama went
to the scene of this orgy and noted down the names of the
besotted traders.   On the Monday following, Khama, with

great moral courage, arraigned them before his court. The missionary J. D. Hepburn was present and reported the scene. Khama challenged the white traders: ' You think you can despise my laws because I am a black man.' He demanded that they leave his country: ' Take everything you have, strip the iron off the roofs, gather all your possessions and go! . . . I am trying to lead my people according to the Word of God, which we have received from you white people, and you show us an example of wickedness.'

His third problem was how to put down witchcraft and rain-making. Well may his biographer, J. C. Harris, ask: ' Has there been in history a more dramatic figure than this son of a sorcerer, standing up in the kraal of his tribe, and bravely breaking with the heathen sanctions and standards of his tribe?'

His responsibilities as chief over a geographical area more than five times the size of England and Wales were immense. In his own person he combined the functions of both Houses of Parliament, of judge and jury, of War Office and Ministry of Agriculture and Education, of Foreign Secretary and Chief of Police, as well as being patriarch and protector of his people.

The day began early with prayer and Khama would be seated in the *kgotla* soon after dawn. In this wide courtyard, ringed about with a stockade of wooden posts and under the shadow of a tree, he would preside over the business of the tribe. Runners came to the chief and his headmen with the news; men with grievances came to report them and to demand compensation; perhaps a European arrived to ask permission to open a store, or a deputation of witch-doctors sought authority for re-establishing the ceremony of initiation. The decision on all these weighty matters had to be the chief's.

Khama also recognized his responsibility over vassal peoples. Many of these (Bushmen, for example) escaped

from conditions of unrelieved serfdom when Khama became chief, as they could now own land and cattle and live
unmolested. The chief even addressed them as 'my
people'. Selous, the famous hunter, declares that the
Bakalahari (subject tribe of the Bamangwato) seemed
'joyless, soulless, hopeless animals' in the pre-Khama days,
but under his influence had become a happy, pastoral
people, transformed almost beyond recognition.

He paid heed to his Christian convictions even when
great pressure was put on him to re-introduce pagan
tribal customs in times of crisis. For instance, during a
searing drought Lobengula sent a message asking Khama to
co-operate in rain-making ceremonies. Khama replied that
he could not see how a 'god' who ate porridge like
himself could be of any use in an emergency!

The country of Bechuanaland was declared a Protectorate in 1885; but at the end of the century Khama was
perturbed at the prospect of the Chartered Company (now
gaining ground in Rhodesia) taking his country under its
rule. Cecil Rhodes urged that the southern portion of the
Protectorate should be annexed by the Cape Colony and
that Khama's country be handed over to the Chartered
Company. Khama felt strongly that the Native policy
of the Company would endanger the freedom of his
subjects. Mackenzie the missionary was of the same
opinion and wrote compellingly to that effect in the pages
of *The Contemporary Review*. In 1895, accompanied by
two of his missionaries, Khama went to England to present
his views before the British Government. So persuasively
did they state their case, and so impressed was Britain
by Khama's wisdom and beneficence, that the cause was
won.

In 1902 Khama obtained the permission of the High
Commissioner to remove the headquarters and capital of
the tribe forty-five miles away to the healthier area of
Serowe. In 1914 the great new stone church was built

and it is a significant testimony to the tribe's appreciation
of Christianity that they raised between £7,000 and £8,000
of the cost of the new building themselves. Khama, as
might be expected, was the most generous contributor.
Another great institution serving Bechuanaland, though
located in the Northern Cape, is also a Christian foundation.* That is Tiger Kloof, the industrial, teacher-
training and theological institution. This Lovedale of
Bechuanaland was a project after Khama's own heart,
for he believed, like Livingstone his first missionary, in
Christianizing and civilizing his people simultaneously.

Perhaps the most outstanding proof of Khama's religious wisdom was his official approval of one missionary
society, the L.M.S., with its catholic policy of bringing
the Gospel to the people, without insistence on episcopacy,
presbytery or independency, leaving their charges to determine for themselves the most suitable form of ecclesiastical polity. He did not allow warring and divisive sects
to propagate their variations and thus bewilder his people.
Thus, there has rarely been in Bechuanaland an unseemly
scramble for ' Christian scalps ' as, for example, in Basutoland. It is abundantly clear that the London Missionary
Society has lifted the Bamangwato out of savagery.

Not the least remarkable aspect of Khama's character
is that he himself was a missionary. He encouraged the
Bamangwato to establish missions among the folk who
lived on the edge of Lake Ngami. His charity towards
the poor of his own people was equally remarkable, for it
was as unostentatious as it was generous. It was, for
example, usual for him to pay the doctor's fees of his
impecunious sick people.

In 1922 the jubilee of the reign of Khama was celebrated. In an historic speech the old chief said: ' I thank
God for the missionaries. They brought us the Light

* Moyeng is a great school, towards which the Bechuana contributed £60,000. It was a dream of Khama's fulfilled in Tshekedi's time.

8

and showed us the Road.' He, too, was a Light-bringer
to his own people. A year later he died at his capital,
while at prayer with his missionary in the early morning.
It could be said of him, ' He has fought the good fight,
finished his course and kept the faith '. Perhaps no African within living memory has so completely vindicated
the potentialities of the Bantu race or won so high a place
in the aristocracy of character. His wisdom, his sense
of responsibility, his fidelity to the Christian standards
and his resolute courage, are beacons of hope in an uncertain future.

CHAPTER XIII

JAMES STEWART

THE life of a man who proved to be Livingstone's friend in a moment of crisis, who was called by Lord Milner ' the greatest human in South Africa ', and who, with Livingstone and Schweitzer, deserves to be called one of the three greatest medical missionaries of Africa, is worth studying. His was a life of boundless energy (the Africans called him *Somgxada*, the long-strider, or the man who is everywhere), of pioneering exploration in Central and East Africa, of ideas translated into action. He was the first medical missionary to found a hospital for Africans, and to train nurses and hospital assistants. The foundation of the first University College for Non-Europeans (Africans, Coloured and Indians) was his idea, and the South African Native College at Fort Hare came into existence only eleven years after his death. He founded the daughter of Lovedale at Blythswood, and pioneered the Church of Scotland mission in Livingstonia (now Nyasaland) which to-day is part of the great Central African Church (in which the Presbyterian mission, the D.R.C. mission and the London Missionary Society have joined forces) and boasts a Christian community of 153,592 souls (1949). He, too, accepted the challenge of the British East African Company and pioneered the Presbyterian mission 200 miles from Mombasa and 40 miles north-east of the snow-crested Kilimanjaro. His missionary classic, entitled *Dawn on the Dark Continent*, is probably the best nineteenth-century text-book on the technique of African missions, and he himself deserves to be called the chief light-bringer. A man of great

112

height and commanding presence, he is the best proof of the saying that ' there were giants amongst us yesterday '. In courage and in the application of Christian conviction to race relationships he was a giant. In his tenure of the Principalship of Lovedale, this institution was the most renowned in Southern Africa, exceeding in fame even the universities. In retrospect, he seems a Christian Colossus: yet no man was less complacent, or more modest. His memorial on Sandile's Kop, overlooking Lovedale, bears the simple but adequate description, JAMES STEWART, MISSIONARY. This missionary took as his charter the famous words of Livingstone: ' God had only one Son, and He was a missionary and a physician. A poor imitation of Him I am, or wish to be.'

This man of Viking stature and Scots sagacity was born in Edinburgh in 1831. His first home was only a stone's throw from Prince's Street and the great rock citadel of Edinburgh Castle. At that time his father was a cab proprietor, who later purchased a farm. His mother was of Norse descent and gentle ways. On the farm between Perth and Scone his father used to hold religious gatherings for those who, like himself, had broken away from the established Church of Scotland in 1843, to found the vigorous Free Church of Scotland, untrammelled by the State yoke. In his early teens Stewart was present at many of the services held in the barnyard in summer and in the barn illuminated by candles in the winter.

His decision to become a missionary was made most solemnly when ploughing a furrow at the age of fifteen. ' God helping me,' he vowed, ' I will be a missionary.' His boyhood dream was to traverse Africa with a Bible in his pocket and a rifle in his hand. Through all his life he followed an adventurous and dangerous Christianity. In this strong frame there was a stout heart; it is recorded that James regularly carried a lame boy to and from church and Sunday school on his back, a distance of a mile. In these years the lad's favourite reading was Plutarch, Shakespeare, Milton and Browning.

When the farm proved a failure, his father returned to Edinburgh in an attempt to recoup the fortunes of the family. James went into business, but contrived to spend most of his spare time as a part-time student in the Science Faculty of the University of Edinburgh. He later took the opportunity of tutoring two of his cousins in St. Andrew's and at the same time of attending the oldest University in Scotland. During these years he was a diligent student of botany, chemistry and agriculture. In 1855 be began studying Divinity in New College, the home of the Faculty of Divinity in Edinburgh University. He had not lost touch with his old love, science, for he published two books on botany whilst studying theology. His *Synopsis of Structural and Physiological Botany* was a text-book widely used for many years.

The renewed impetus and re-consecration to the missionary vocation came when he read Livingstone's *Travels and Researches in South Africa,* which was published in 1857. In 1860 Stewart was licensed as a probationer minister of the Free Church of Scotland. During this time he held temporary appointments in various congregations, and attended classes in the faculty of medicine from 1859-61.

In the latter year he took up Livingstone's challenge to keep open the door of missions in Africa and, although almost unknown, he galvanized an impressive committee of eighteen men into action as ' The New Central Africa Committee '. On their recommendation it was decided that Stewart should go to Central Africa as a missionary prospector, to report on the possibility of establishing missions in that area.

On 6 July 1861, he set sail from Southampton in the *Celt.* One of his most important duties was to escort Mary Livingstone to her husband. They reached Cape

Town on 13 August, and there his difficulties commenced.
Several persons tried to damp his enthusiasm by describing
his attempt as foolhardy and his ignorance of African
conditions as almost criminal.   Rumours were spread that
he was an unscrupulous trader in missionary guise.
Another Church resented the implication that Central
Africa was not exclusively its own missionary territory.
Indeed, it was only Mrs. Livingstone's obdurate advocacy
of his cause that enabled him to obtain a berth on a Glasgow brig leaving Port Natal on 24 December. He was
in no mood to celebrate Christmas aboard the ship.

On 1 February 1862, he met his hero, Livingstone, on
the Zambezi. Five months later he wrote of this encounter:
'It seemed to me the realizing of some strange dream to be
rambling through the grassy delta and mangrove forests
of the Zambezi on this African summer evening with
Livingstone.' Stewart was adaptable and his vision of
traversing Africa with a gun in one hand and a Bible in
the other was quickly realized. He had to shoot for the
pot, or there would have been no meat. He wrote: 'I
could not but think it a curious phenomenon in my life
that here in the heavy tropical twilight I should be
stumping about among muddy creeks, wet up the knees
among tall reeds and grass on an alligator-haunted island
in search of something for to-morrow's dinner.' He
managed to travel light —'a piece of soap, a towel and a
comb' completed his luggage. He could not afford to
wait for the start of Livingstone's expedition into the
interior, and so, accompanied only by another missionary
and some African assistants he pushed on.

In this remarkable journey his means of transport was
a canoe fashioned out of the trunk of a tree. This was
steered through rivers abounding in sandbanks, rapids,
whirlpools, crocodiles and hippopotami. In the pestiferous
'Elephants Marsh' they came across a hunter's paradise
— herds of up to three hundred elephants at a time. On

one island they counted seventy-two alligators basking in
the sun. They passed the Murchison cataracts and explored
the hill country to the east of the Shiré, where the Blantyre mission now stands, and remarked on the healthiness
and fertility of this land.   Dauntlessly he entered the
African villages, although the inhabitants had never before
seen a white man.   Each night he talked simply to them
about Jesus the Christ 'a phrase never heard by them
before'.   He was convinced of the practicability of establishing missions here, but it was many years before he was
able to accomplish his design.   Despite the exhaustion and
almost complete physical disintegration of the man, he
reported to the Scottish Committee that the project was
practicable.   The spirit of the man is revealed in his
dietetic comment: 'a man with a good sound appetite
would enjoy a roast sirloin of hippopotamus'.

The most solemn memory he kept of this expedition was
of Shupanga in April 1862, when Mary Livingstone was
dying.   Livingstone and Kirk knelt in the room, while
Stewart commended her soul to God.   David Livingstone
found his Christian and scientific friend a great tower of
strength in this time of testing.

Stewart returned to Edinburgh and completed his
medical studies.   Then he offered himself as a missionary
of the Free Church of Scotland at their Eastern Province
institution Lovedale, with the proviso that he could go to
the Central African work if that were to open up.   He
returned to Africa, having married the gracious Miss Mina
Stephen, who was to share his interests through the years.

In 1870, at the age of thirty-nine, he became the second
Principal of Lovedale.   There he shaped the life of the
institution on a fourfold policy.   He aimed to train
preachers, intellectually and spiritually fit young men
among the Coloured and Africans; he planned to provide
well-equipped teachers for Native schools.   He determined
to train a number of Natives for trades and crafts, such

as printing, wagon-making, blacksmithing, carpentering, bookbinding, general agricultural work, and telegraph clerks. He was equally convinced that Lovedale must provide a general education in which Africans and Europeans should share. His defence, in view of the contrary theories held in the Union to-day, is most illuminating. 'All colours mingle freely there, as force of brain rather than colour of skin determines the position. The Natives carry off their own share of the prizes. The Europeans sit in the same dining-hall, but at different tables, and they sleep in different dormitories. The objects gained by thus mixing the two races are these:— The Natives have the advantage of contact with the Europeans for the language and general competition. And many of the Europeans, I might say nearly all, gain a lasting sympathy with the Natives and acquire an interest in missions.'

When Stewart's critics insisted that the white man would lose the respect of the Africans by such a policy, his reply was that those who deserved it would get it! An administrator, medical man, and minister, he certainly deserved the appreciation of the Africans and they gave it unstintedly.

During the thirty-five years he was at the head of Lovedale it made phenomenal advances and was the pattern missionary institution for Africa, many others paying it the tribute of imitation. Often Stewart was absent from Lovedale, but on every occasion in the interest of missions. In the seventh decade of the century he concentrated on establishing the daughter missionary institution at Blythswood, the story of which is a saga of Fingo giving, for these Africans contributed over £4,500 towards the cost of the buildings. In the eighth decade of the century Stewart was pioneering the Church of Scotland mission in Nyasaland. In the ninth decade he was pioneering the East African mission.

In these years he was honoured far beyond the confines
of his adopted country. In 1892 and 1893, for example,
he was invited to accept a lectureship on Evangelistic
Theology, and he taught ministerial and missionary
students in the Universities of Edinburgh, Glasgow and
Aberdeen. In 1893 Glasgow gave him its Honorary Doctorate of Divinity. In 1899 his Church accorded him its
chief honour, by calling him to the Moderatorship of the
General Assembly. He was the first missionary in Africa
and the second physician to be honoured in this way.

His fame was being spread by his books, also. His
Lovedale, Past and Present was, according to the present
Principal of Lovedale (Dr. R. H. W. Shepherd), an
entirely new type of missionary propaganda. It was pre-
dominantly statistical and allowed the results to speak
for themselves. His *Dawn on the Dark Continent*, which
incorporated the lectures he gave in Scotland on the Duff
Missionary Foundation, was a brilliant survey of the strategy of missions in Southern Africa. *The Christian Express*, a periodical printed and published at Lovedale and
founded by Stewart, was known as ' *The Spectator* of
South Africa '.

The acclaim of his colleagues was made known when,
in 1904, he was asked to preside over the first South African General Missionary Conference. He was a prophet
with honour in his own and his adopted country. Perhaps
the most remarkable feature of this man who stood six
feet two inches high, and who as explorer, missionary,
medical man, educationalist, and author, had been a
pioneer, was his compassion for individuals. This was
seen in the case of the small European boy who had been
bitten by a snake, from whose body Stewart sucked the
poison with his own lips; or in the case of the old leper
for whom Stewart made a cabin beside his house. Moreover, Stewart had the humility of the truly great servant

of Christ, recognizing how great a debt he owed and his own life as too short a span in which to repay it.

Lovedale Hospital, Livingstonia, the South African Native College at Fort Hare, and his place in the history and affections of South Africans of all races, are a better monument even than the eighty-foot memorial raised to him on Sandile's Kop. The most fitting comment on his life is that made by his biographer, Dr. James Wells: ' God's greatest gifts are men fitted for the needs of their age, and a life like this does more to enrich a land than mines of gold and diamonds can. It is a rebuke and an inspiration to the average man, and it should increase our respect . . . for the faith to which James Stewart owed all his noblest qualities and achievements.'

CHAPTER XIV

FRANÇOIS COILLARD

THE alternative title for this biography might well have
been ' a study in determination '. No missionary pioneer has ever lived more completely by faith, as distinct
from walking by sight, than Coillard. He was a triumphant failure: by that I mean he could see few results of his
sowing of the seed of the Gospel among the Barotse when
he died, yet he was confident of ultimate success because
of the fidelity of His Lord. For him, however badly the
campaign seemed to be going, the one thing needful was
obedience. ' Obedience is the politeness of a soldier.' Apart
from this superb endurance, Coillard had many other
qualities. He was a gifted poet, singer, translator, explorer, and to read of his denunciations of Lewanika, king
of the Barotse, is like being present at Nathan's condemn-
ation of King David. He was a prophet, as well as an
evangelist: he fulfilled both duties superbly because of his
knowledge of the Divine Revelation and of the customs and
the language of a primitive people. As a missionary, his
techniques were original and brilliant, and he had the
inspired faculty of seeing the best in the most degraded
of people. Moreover, he saw individuals as souls, not
as statistics or missionary scalps.

In his fascinating life we are always meeting the unexpected. ' With God ', said Coillard, ' we are never certain what is going to happen.' Nor with this servant of
God. He was apprenticed in the service of an English
clergyman, Kirby, in his manor of thirty farms in Föecy
in France, a few miles away from his birthplace, Asnières.
Often he was found asleep at his job. Instead of ex-

pulsion, the clergyman called the boy's minister and a local schoolmaster to advise him, and they sent him away to Glay, an institution where boys of slender means were prepared for the ministry or teaching. When he had completed his training, one would have predicted for this sensitive, introspective and patriotic ordinand, a career as a scholarly country parson — certainly not a foot-slogging campaign for Christ in South Africa, beneath the British flag! Again, the unexpected took place when Coillard, who should have returned to France on long-overdue leave, decided to lead the expedition of the Paris Evangelical Missionary Society beyond the Zambezi.

Many strands of tradition and environment were interwoven to produce the sensitive and complex personality of François Coillard. The chief influences on his life were his courageous widowed mother; M. Bost, the French Reformed minister, and his daughter; M. Jaquet, the Principal of Glay; the example and the writings of Robert Moffat; a sermon of Bishop Ryle's; and the leadership of M. Eugène Casalis and the close friendship of Adolphe Mabille. From his mother he received an example of determination even in penury, and an account of the exploits of the Huguenots. M. Bost was a minister in the proud Puritan tradition who locked the church at the hour when service began so as to teach the lingering elders the importance of keeping a punctual rendezvous with God. In his short, ten-minute sermons he illustrated the deadly sins by examples drawn from his congregation actually sitting before him. He was respected, but his daughter was loved. She used to read to the young people the sagas of modern missions, and early on in his life Robert Moffat became young François's hero. Mlle Bost also taught them to sing the praises of God in lively, haunting measures, banishing solemnity and melancholy with her gay Christian spirit. Perhaps the greatest debt François owed to M. Jaquet, his Principal, was due to that man's modesty as a preacher.   It seems that the Principal knew he was a poor preacher and one Sunday he substituted for a sermon the reading of a pamphlet by the evangelical Bishop Ryle of Liverpool.   The effect on Coillard was electric, as may be seen in his own words:

> I was miserable, I wriggled like a worm; I cursed inwardly this M. Ryle this unknown disturber of my peace, and this good M. Jaquet, who not knowing how to preach (so I reasoned) borrowed the sermons of somebody or other!   When the reading was ended and the question had been put for the last time ['Are you wheat or chaff?'], it seemed to me that a vast silence fell and the whole world waited for an answer.   It was an awful moment.   And this moment, a veritable hell, seemed to last for ever.

The thunders of Sinai had shaken the formality and complacency of Coillard and he was now experiencing the dark night of the soul — the agonizing moments before the dawn of the love of Christ.   Thus the deepest experience of his spiritual life was produced by a sermon borrowed from an English bishop read haltingly out to a French boy.   Incalculable!

His sense of vocation to the missionary life was now a firm conviction and so he offered himself to the Directors of the Paris Evangelical Missionary Society.   They sent him for further training, first to Magny in the Jura country, where he slaved at his New Testament in Greek and learned some Latin and a little Hebrew (all of which were to be invaluable to the future translator of Scriptures into primitive languages).   He then had four further years of training in Paris and Strasbourg.   He developed a great love for natural history at Strasbourg and his tutor was so impressed by his ability that he urged him to consider a career devoted to science.   In Paris he found the Head of the House of Missions, Dr. Eugène Casalis, Sr., most inspiring in his wide knowledge of missions, for he had returned after many years of pioneering work in Basutoland. There another great missionary-to-be, Adolphe Mabille, and he were bosom friends. Coillard was already renowned for his eloquence, and his comrades nicknamed him 'Chrysostom' (the golden-mouthed). The same eloquence must have won the heart of Christina Mackintosh, the daughter of an Edinburgh minister, who was staying with friends in Paris. François often recalled a sublime evening when the streets of Paris were crowded for the illuminations in honour of the Emperor and he was Christina's escort. He did not dare to propose to her in those days, because of the uncertainties of his calling, but when he wrote a few years later from his lonely hermitage at Leribé in Basutoland, Christina accepted him. In these student days he worked hard at his books, attended the services conducted by that great preacher Adolphe Monod (with his seraphic expression and dramatic gifts), and entered avidly into wild undergraduate jests. He was overjoyed when Dr. Casalis informed him, one morning, that the Directors of the Society wished him to proceed to Basutoland.

After a bitter parting from his mother who said: 'Adieu, my son, I shall not see you again', he sailed for the Cape on 2 September 1857 in the *Trafalgar*, hardly the name a patriotic Frenchman would have chosen for his ship! He reached Cape Town on 6 November. A few months later he was in Hermon mission station learning Sotho, and not long afterwards he went to the lonely station of Leribé, which was to be his home for nearly twenty years. Mme Mabille wrote of these years:

> Few young missionaries have had a lonelier life or one of more entire self-sacrifice than his during the three years he passed there alone, before Mme Coillard came out to him — surrounded by an entirely heathen population, hearing

nothing from morning till night, and often all night through, but the wild shouts, the din of their heathen dances, their drunken brawls. His food at that time consisted of native bread with thick milk and pumpkin. I remember him spending days knee-deep in water, cutting the reeds with which to cover his first little cottage. At that time there was not a single Christian in the whole district with whom to hold Christian fellowship.

There, forty-four miles from the nearest mission station, he learned the art of missionary independence. In this way he had to learn the language and the customs of the Basuto and some Basuto he came to know very intimately. A great friend was Nathanael Makatoko, nephew of Moshesh, a legendary figure known for his exploits as a warrior, but who combined generosity to the beaten and the weak with great daring. Makatoko became as faithful a Christian as he had been a soldier and it was a great delight to Coillard when he visited the exiled missionary in Natal many years later. His friendship made up for the duplicity of Molapo, the chief of the Leribé district.

In 1859 the missionary built his first cottage. It was 25 feet long, by 12 feet wide, by 7 feet high, and consisted of three rooms: one for dining and reception, one for his bed, and the third his study, where the photographs of his friends in Europe had pride of place. The home was dedicated by killing and roasting an ox and inviting his people to share in the feast. He had a real instinct for ceremony which endeared him to the Basuto.

His technique as a missionary was brilliant. He had mastered the proverbial lore and vivid expressions of Sotho and he took his place as adviser in the *khotla*. In his preaching he made great use of fables in the manner of Aesop and La Fontaine. How effective this was may be realized from an entry in his diary for 26 March and from the testimony of missionaries that these fables are retold and re-enacted by children in Basutoland to this day.

The entry reads: 'I preached upon Luke XIII, 1. I recounted the fable of the Grasshopper, the Ant and the Bee, imitated from *La Cigale et la Fourmi*. It seemed to produce some effect, for after worship some groups were formed in which they repeated what I said.' He also won his way to the heart of the people by writing not merely hymns, but Christian songs for national and tribal occasions. He even provided short snatches of songs which the Basuto could repeat when ploughing and reaping. They loved to ask him to ' weep ' on his accordion! He believed and proved that poetry and song are two rungs of the ladder leading to God.

On the 3 January 1861, he set out to meet Christina. He was despondent on learning that her ship was not coming from the Cape to Port Elizabeth, as he had first been told. So he rode through four days and nights, proving that his fair lady had no faint-heart for a lover. They were married in Union Church, Cape Town, by the Rev. A. Fauré, a friendly minister of the Dutch Reformed Church. She was brilliant and practical, while he was sensitive and imaginative; they were everything to each other. Christina made their wagon a home, with attractive curtains, rugs and even plants. Her husband wrote: ' It is the eighth wonder of the world.' It was a symbol of their wayfaring life — their life together was to be more mobile than that of most missionaries.

On reaching Leribé, François dubbed the house the ' Ex-Hermitage '. The first five years of their married life were spent here. No children were born to them, but the Basuto became their adopted children. Christina started a school and François busied himself with evangelism, teaching and translating the Book of Proverbs into Sotho. He was pleased to find that the Basuto had coined proverbs of their own which the wise men of Israel might have delighted in. One of them was, 'A horse may stumble though it has four paws', and another, 'The child of the crab walks sideways'.

So their simple, arduous life continued, but not without a few pangs of homesickness. Christina, seeing that this was worrying her husband, settled the account with herself by burning all her letters from home. She met François at the door, saying: 'I have burnt them all. You shall never see me fretting any more. Forget thine own people and thy father's house.' François braved many perils from men and nature in these years, but he stated his *credo* thus: 'My work is not done, and until it is done I am immortal.'

In April 1866, during the war between the Free State and Basutoland, the missionaries were ordered to leave Basutoland with all their belongings. Molapo, the chief of their area, was thought to have betrayed and maligned them to the Boers.* It is certain that he pillaged their goods and established himself in the mission house near Leribé. With a heavy heart they left for Natal.

The Coillards took over the work of an American missionary at Ifumi. This was an attractive place and gave them glimpses of ships sailing past to the Indies. They were able to live more sociable lives and to procure books in this healing interlude. Though they disapproved of his unorthodox theology, they learned to appreciate Bishop Colenso, who lent them books and offered them the hospitality of his home. On one visit they were stupefied to hear a Zulu, to whom the Bishop introduced them, saying: 'Don't you know me? I am the Zulu who converted Colenso.' Life was much more interesting in Natal than in Basutoland, but their hearts were with their previous charges.

---

* Molapo was unjustly suspected in this instance.

After two years, they were sent by their Society to Motito, their sole station in the northern Cape. Their short stay here enabled them to see a good deal of their hero, Dr. Robert Moffat, now an ageing veteran. They also learned to know Roger Price, his son-in-law.

In 1869 they were overjoyed to return to Leribé, and to discover that many of their charges had remained faithful to the Christian faith under great temptations to apostasy. Here they stayed for five more years and might have remained in Basutoland to the end of their days had not the unexpected intervened in the person of Major Malan, an envoy from the parent Society in Paris. At a missionary conference in King William's Town he urged them to undertake further missionary work and that was the beginning of the Barotseland Mission with which the Coillards were to be identified in the eyes of the missionary world for the rest of their days.

But first they had to find a new territory and a chief who would welcome them! As it happened, they saw one door after another on their first expedition closed in their faces. From 1877 to 1879 Coillard had the humiliating experience of being an unwanted missionary. Once it was only his calm confidence that prevented his entire party from being massacred by the men of Masonda, chief of the Banyai in the northern Transvaal. Lobengula in Bulawayo also rejected them, but while here they learned that there was a Sotho-speaking tribe on the far banks of the Zambezi, which seemed a happy augury. Barotseland appeared the inevitable destination.

Their first joyful reception was at the hands of Khama, the great Christian chief of the Bamangwato, in Shoshong. He provided them with messengers and the party set off for Barotseland, Christina in a litter and her niece, Elise, on a donkey. They travelled through a vast waterless desert, until at the end of July 1878 they pitched camp at Leshona, which was for months their resting-place on the

southern banks of the Zambezi. Here they learned that
the Barotse were at war and Khama's messengers were
arrested by the Barotse chief, Lewanika. When he
released the envoys, he instructed them to tell the missionary to come in the following June when he should have
completed his capital town. There was nothing for it but
to return. They came back via Valdézia, the headquarters
of the Swiss Mission in the northern Transvaal. In this
neighbourhood they received their next rebuff, this time
at the hands of the famous rain queen, Mujaji, who refused
to have missionaries in her tribe. Before trekking through
the Transvaal they had fallen in with Serpa Pinto, the
famous Portuguese traveller, whom they nursed back to
health. His testimonial to Coillard is worth citing, for it
takes one brave man to recognize another. Pinto wrote:
' François Coillard is the best, kindest man I ever came
across. To a superior intelligence he unites an indomitable
will.' Coillard returned, a very disappointed man, to
Basutoland; he had been rejected and despised by four
different chiefs in his long, wearisome journey. None the
less, he begged the missionary Synod to let him go back
to the Zambezi immediately. They, however, urged that
he should first return to France to obtain missionary
recruits and new financial resources for the Zambezi
mission.

He and his wife returned to their native lands, France
and Scotland, to find themselves famous. They travelled
to Holland, Belgium, Piedmont and England to plead for
their work. They proved a most popular missionary
deputation, and a successful one.

The second journey to Barotseland was undertaken in
1884, when Coillard was fifty. It was three years later
before he was able to escort his wife to their first home
in Barotseland. The tribe had its hands figuratively and
actually dripping with gore. Plots and counter-revolutions
were the bloody orders of the day. If human nature was

degraded, Mother Nature was impressive in her colour, variety and force. They saw enormous herds of antelope which were stranded on muddy islands in the Zambezi, whenever the floods advanced. There were elands, lions, zebras, monkeys, hippopotami and crocodiles in plenty. The ibis, the heron, the pelican and the crane flourished, as did also the warrior ants, locusts and tsetse flies. Lealui, the capital of the Barotse, was in ruins, for the rebel under-chiefs had made common cause against the tyrannical Lewanika, defeated him and placed a boy and puppet-king on the throne. In 1886, however, he regained his suzerainty and invited Coillard to meet him. Lewanika, despite his bloodthirsty cunning, was most courteous to the missionary, treating him like a brother potentate. Coillard ate a meal of royal goose with him and was taken in a royal procession in the leading canoe up the river to the sound of drums, with occasional halts at the ancestral tomb of the past kings. The great tragedy of Coillard's life was that for all his love, patience and skill in applying the Word of God, he was unable to win Lewanika to the allegiance of Christ. None the less, the first station was established at Sesheke, and the work of teaching and preaching was begun.

It must be remembered that a pioneer missionary to a primitive tribe faces a gigantic task. He has to be a teacher, evangelist, craftsman, exemplar of Christianity and civilization, maker of a new literature, as well as prophet and nation-builder. On several occasions Coillard risked his life in standing for justice against the cruelty of the king towards one of his scapegoats. Once, Liomba — one of the king's ministers — came wrongly under Lewanika's suspicions. He was forced to leave his place in the shade, to strip himself of all his garments, to crouch down in the midst of the *pitso* quite alone on the burning sand, whilst the crowd shrieked at him. The mob cried

that he should be bound with cords and slain. The official
protector of accused persons would not move a finger to
protect him. But for Coillard's intervention he was as
good as dead. Shouting above the din, the missionary
cried: ' Barotse, a servant of God is a *Natamoyo*, a minister
of mercy. You shall not kill that man; you can kill me
first.'

Another incident exhibits the cool courage of Coillard.
In his sixty-second year he determined to make an expedition up the river. All went well until he and his
Native travellers encountered Kakenge, a rebellious vassal
chief who owed allegiance to Lewanika. His men treated
Coillard's men with contempt and drove them away. Some
of the hot-blooded wanted to attack immediately; others
urged instant flight. The missionary rejected both methods,
adding: ' The heart of Kakenge is as much in the hands of
God as that of Lewanika. . . . To-morrow Kakenge
will not only send food but will give us words of peace.'

The morning broke, after a night without attack; but
the noon and most of the afternoon passed without the
promised deliverance. At last, at about 3 o'clock, a procession advanced towards them bearing baskets of manioc,
millet, sweet potatoes and fowls from Kakenge! The
prophet and his God were vindicated. As it happened, to
have followed either of the courses proposed by the Barotse
would have led to certain death, for Kakenge had posted
his warriors to watch all avenues of escape. Because the
party waited, the chief Kakenge believed in their pacific
intentions and he begged them to return in the following
year. Twelve members of the expedition were so impressed
by this proof that God answers prayer that on their
return they publicly professed themselves Christians.

The latter years of Coillard were shadowed by sorrow
and bereavement. In 1891 his beloved Christina died
and was buried on the banks of the Zambezi — as was
Mary Livingstone. Fever took its toll of his assistants;

Lewanika was friendly but unwilling to accept the faith for himself (though his sons did so); and the Ethiopian Movement, assisted by one of his former colleagues, caused much disaffection among the members of the Native Christian community. But throughout the work of establishing new stations, building houses and schools, translating and preaching continued. Coillard returned to Europe in 1896 for further reinforcements and such was the magnetic compulsion of the man that he came back to the Zambezi in 1898 with a convoy of 21 wagons and 80 persons (including 15 new missionaries).

Arm-chair critics in South Africa and overseas wondered if the field was not too difficult or, perhaps, too remote from the other French Reformed stations. To such he replied:

> Do people seriously think that we are capable of deserting a post, because it is perilous above all others? It is the Cross, yes, the Cross with its sufferings and shame that has redeemed the world and since in Christianity Jesus and His Cross are not to be separated, let us thank God that here it is given to us to know both.

He endured valiantly, ' as seeing Him Who is invisible ', to the end. The faithful Barotse, hearing that their missionary was gravely ill and likely to die, surrounded his mission house and sang with hushed voices a translation of the hymn ' Sur Toi je me repose ' (' On Thee my soul reposes '). His body was carried down the great river ceremonially to such music.

His last look upon earth in 1904 was on scenes of failure almost unredeemed, but his faith in the possibility of making splendid Christians of the Barotse was undimmed. It breathes in his last will and testament made out to the executors, the Protestant Churches of France, the successors of the Huguenots:

On the threshold of eternity and in the presence of my God, I solemnly bequeath to the Churches of France, my native land, the responsibility of the Lord's work in Barotseland, and I adjure them in His Holy Name, never to give it up — which would be to despise and renounce the rich harvest reserved to the sowing they have accomplished in suffering and tears.

The faith of this gallant Christian gentleman has been honoured.

CHAPTER XV

JAN LION CACHET

WHAT a colourful personality Ds. Jan Lion Cachet was! Interests that in other men would have been incompatible were welded into the unity of his personality: a Jew by race, a Christian by conviction, an Afrikaner by adoption, and a puritan, a poet and a theological professor, all in one. To many, perhaps, the most remarkable amalgam in him was that of poetry and puritanism. It might be thought that a *predikant* of the ' Doppers ' (the *Gereformeerde Kerk*) would have despised fiction, far less have proved himself to be a catholic connoisseur and critic of novels and poetry, and, least of all, a writer. In fact however, he saw no incongruity between celebrating the triumphs of grace and the beauties of nature and human nature, equally the gifts of the One Creator. In this appreciation of puritanism and poetry he had several distinguished predecessors and at least one successor. For Milton and Vondel were two outstanding examples of the fusion of Geneva and Athens, and Prof. J. P. du Toit ('Totius'), has followed Ds. Cachet's example in the *Gereformeerde Kerk* with even greater distinction.

Dr. P. J. Nienaber, who has written of him in an attractive short biography (*Jan Lion Cachet met sy Sewe Duiwels*), claims that Cachet was distinguished as a founder of the Church, as an educationalist, as a writer, as a teacher and professor of theology, and as an early protagonist of the Afrikaans language. This mere catalogue is an indication of his many-sided importance.

This great-hearted servant of Christ and of his adopted Afrikaner people was born in 1838 in Amsterdam. The

family was Lion and they rejoiced in deriving their ancestry from the tribe of Levi. The second surname, Cachet
(meaning ' seal '), was assumed by his ancestors in France,
when Napoleon I insisted upon all French citizens adopting
a French surname. It was his grandfather, a prominent
engraver, who left France to seek for new opportunities
in the jewel and precious metal trades which Amsterdam
offered.

This gentleman was equally averse to the faith of his
fathers and to the Christian faith, until he met the brilliant former Jew and Christian apologist, Isaac da Costa.
The encounter with this enthusiastic Christian and poet
led to the baptism of the entire Cachet family in the
Noorder Kerk in Amsterdam.

The boy Jan was educated in da Costa's school, where he
learned to admire the deep faith and philanthropy of his
leader and the lyrical poetry which he wrote. Da Costa
was, in short, his hero, and for many years his portrait
was placed in a prominent position in Cachet's study. In
1857 Jan sat and passed his teacher's examination, and two
years later was appointed an approved catechist and
teacher in the service of the Church. For a time he taught
in the ' Ragged School ' of Amsterdam, where he developed an enduring compassion for the waifs and strays of
our humanity.

His attention was first drawn to South Africa as a field
of Christian service when the *Nederduitse Gereformeerde
Kerk* sent through Dr. Robertson an appeal to Britain and
Holland for recruits for the ministry and the teaching
profession. He responded and reached the Cape in January 1861. For the best part of a year he taught in the
Dutch Reformed Church school in Bree Street, Cape Town.
He then made his way to Natal, for he was anxious to
join his brother, Ds. Frans Lion Cachet, who was minister
of the Dutch Church in Ladysmith. Here he ran his
own school for some time, and, during a vacation, visited

Basutoland, where he was greatly impressed by the work of the Paris Evangelical Missionary Society. Of an incident in this visit, namely meeting with Moshesh, he recalls that it was the only time in his life when he was waited on at table by a king!

The decisive year of his life was 1865. He then made the momentous resolution to leave the powerful and impressive D.R.C. to join the ranks of the then small and despised *Gereformeerde Kerk*, which had been founded only six years before by Ds. Postma. Jan Lion Cachet was deeply impressed by the convictions and the integrity of the founder of the ' Doppers ', believing, with him, that modernism and liberalism would rive the very foundations of the older Church.

Ds. Postma was then the minister of the Rustenburg congregation and Cachet received his theological training at his hands, along with a number of other ordinands. He might be described as one of Postma's assistants, or perhaps, as his aide-de-camp: for they both travelled far to outlying farms. In these days his study was the ox-wagon, as John Wesley's was the back of a horse. However rudimentary the instruction was in this mobile theological college, at least it did not expose the students to the danger of preferring books to living epistles, people!

In 1866 Ds. Postma was called to minister to the Burghersdorp congregation, and his ministerial students, Cachet included, followed him. In the same year the Rustenburg congregation asked Lion Cachet to return as their minister on the completion of his studies. The future President Kruger happened to be one of the signatories of this letter. In July 1868 he was ordained and inducted as minister of this congregation. Only a month before he had cemented his deep friendship with Professor Postma by marrying his daughter Zwaantjie.

In 1869 he was invited to become a lecturer in the newly-formed Theological School of Burghersdorp, and the second minister of the congregation. From this humble beginning arose the Theological School of Potchefstroom, and thence the Potchefstroom University College for Christian Higher Education, which has recently attained the status of a separate university. Ds. Cachet was to be associated with Burghersdorp for the greater part of his ministerial life. He remained there from 1869 to 1875, and returned there in 1892 as acting Professor of Theology. The intervening years were spent in charge of congregations in Philipstown and Steynsburg.

On the death of Ds. Postma in 1890, Ds. Jan Lion Cachet was the acknowledged leader of the *Gereformeerde Kerk*. He had won this position by his sheer loving kindness and practical sagacity. Like the Pastor of pastors, this under-shepherd went in search of his wandering sheep. Sometimes the flock wandered several hundred miles! In February of 1877, when three hundred Transvaalers began the long trek to Damaraland and halted on the banks of the Crocodile River, he was called from Philipstown to minister to their spiritual needs. Here he established the famous 'Trekking Congregation' of South Africa. Had it not been that the trekkers were unable to spare a wagon and a span of oxen, Ds. Cachet would have gone the whole way with them through the Great Thirstland.

His practical interest in the Transvaal trekkers was again shown in 1881. He undertook the long journey by sea and land to Angola in West Africa and was accorded a royal welcome when he reached the trekkers in the town of Humpata, where he baptized the children and received the new members into the fellowship of the Church.

This devout and lovable pastor was always at the service of his people. He was everyman's philosopher, guide and friend. In Burghersdorp the municipality sought his advice when any new project was under consideration. If there was an important issue at stake, the lawyers would confer with him. If anyone had asked for a loan, then ' Oubaas ' had to give his opinion as to whether security was good. ' Ministers and parliamentary leaders sought his advice — directors of people's organizations took his advice — presidents and generals held councils-of-war in his presence.'

This Grand Old Man of the *Gereformeerde Kerk* received the greatest distinction of his life when the jubilee of the foundation of the Church was celebrated in 1909 at Rustenburg. There he was invested as a Knight of the Order of Orange-Nassau. Three years later he died, mourned by many ministers whom he trained for their calling, by many teachers whom he had encouraged in their privileged vocation, and, most of all, by many whom he had never met, whom he had introduced into the realms of literature.

His own Church will, of course, always revere his memory as its second founder and father-in-God, and as its distinguished theological teacher; but South Africa as a whole will probably remember him longest as a founder of the Afrikaans language and literature, and as the author of *The Seven Devils*.

To that enduring aspect of his work and fame we must now turn. As he loved all types and conditions of people, so was his taste in literature truly catholic. He had a passionate love for poetry and was reputed to be a walking anthology. It is said that he could recite from memory many of the poems of Vondel and van Hooft, of Helmers, Bilderdyk and da Costa. He was an enthusiastic reader of novels and had a great admiration for the works of Wolff and Samuel Richardson. He declared that he preached the most effective sermon in his life after finishing Hawthorne's famous *Scarlet Letter*. His chief delight and his favourite author was W. M. Thackeray (' *mijn lieve-*

lingsboeken '). It seems that he regarded Thackeray's characterization as unrivalled, as also his ethical insight.

He was more than a connoisseur and critic; he was a literary creator. He was, moreover, a builder of the Afrikaans language and literature. He was largely instrumental in founding the first Afrikaans magazine, under the modest and sentimental title of *Ons Klyntjie*. Although he wrote in English and Nederlands, his best poetry was written in Afrikaans. For him this language was the symbol of nationhood, a living proof that the Afrikaner people had their own contribution to make in their own tongue. One of his better-known poems is an allegory on the history and future of the Afrikaans language. His attachment to this language can best be indicated by a citation from the poem in translation (though the translation unfortunately transmutes its simplicity into naïveté):

> A humble farmer's wife am I
> By many thought despicable,
> And yet I come from noble blood
> And ancestry respectable;
> My father from Holland
> To sunlit Africa was bound,
> From France my lovely mother came
> Where swelling grapes are found.

In his hands Afrikaans became the trumpet of patriotism, whether in verse or prose, in lyric or in satire.

In the *Patriot* he produced a number of literary cartoons in the column headed ' Little Black Pills '. He was the doctor prescribing remedies for the national ills of the people, and, while his diagnoses were often acute and witty, his remedies were sometimes as drastic as the disease he discovered. These topical articles will, like most propaganda, prove to be his least enduring work.

His two historical novels, written in Nederlands, deserve to be better known. One of them, *The Family of the Huguenots*, describes the deep convictions and the sufferings of the French Protestants who rediscovered that the Church is an anvil that will wear out many hammers.

His most enduring work, however, is *The Seven Devils and what they did*. This appeared in seven parts (in diabolical sections, in fact!) from 1882 to 1899, and they were collected and published in 1907. The book is a moral and spiritual allegory which invites comparison with Bunyan's *Pilgrim's Progress*, in its fascinating picaresque narrative and realistic descriptions and observations. In vigour of imagination and sustained characterization, however, it is inferior to Bunyan. But as social historians of seventeenth-century England turn to Bunyan's epic, so will social historians of the late nineteenth century in South Africa find Cachet's story a useful quarry. Like every allegory of a religious kind the book is a cleverly gilded pill and it succeeds in that most difficult of tasks — making goodness attractive, and vice despicable. The moralist and literary historian will recognize the stock character of the miser, the shrewish wife, the braggart, the hypocrite, and the scandal-monger, among many others. But he will also appreciate that Jan Lion Cachet has given these abstractions the rich blood of life. Oom Jan van der Lingen the hoarder, Tante Andriana the killer of reputations, Oom Hermanus, green-eyed with jealousy, and Oom Arnoldus, bully and arch-hypocrite, are vivid incarnations of some of the seven deadly sins. They are not, however, limned with the satirist's savage acid, but painted with the kindly brush of a whimsical artist. For the writer wrote as he preached: he hated the vice and liked the sinner. His incidents have all the realism and topsy-turvydom of country life. It is not surprising that the book had reached a twelfth edition by 1924 and that it was prescribed in many South African schools.

The *Gereformeerde Kerk,* which now has a community of over 60,000 souls, was indeed happy in having so convinced a Christian, so compassionate a greatheart, and so imaginative a writer, in the formative years of its history. That they should have received a gift of a Pastor-Poet twice in a century is an enviable heritage.

CHAPTER XVI

STEFANUS HOFMEYR

THE Hofmeyrs are a family of distinction including in their annals a foundation Professor at Stellenbosch Theological Seminary and a Deputy-Prime Minister; but possibly their greatest honour is to have produced the first Afrikaner missionary, Stefanus Hofmeyr, who was not only a pioneer but a perfect missionary. No higher testimonial could be given to him than the words of Robert Moffat, himself a prince of missionaries. Moffat wrote: ' What we hear of him makes us envious.' Professor J. du Plessis, the distinguished historian of missions, who is never given to exaggerated statements, declares, ' he was an ideal missionary '. To few South Africans (especially missionaries) has it been given to be honoured alike by the Afrikaner and the African, but Stefanus Hofmeyr was one of them.

His boyhood was certainly not that of the orthodox missionary, and he was not far wrong in describing himself as the ' leading horse of the devil's team ' (*'n voorperd van die duiwel*). He was born in Cape Town in 1839, one of the nine children of Advocate Hofmeyr. Nothing gave him more pleasure than the look of anxiety on his mother's face when, with clothes tattered past mending, he shouted to her from a tree-top or rode astride a cow as his steed. School made little impression on him, no more indeed than the cane did! He seems to have developed a hide like a rhinoceros and been immune from the effects of thrashings. Dr. Dale, the headmaster of the Cape Town school which he attended, interviewed him alone one day, saying, 'Why are you wild and wicked?

141

If you would only concentrate on your studies, no child could hold a candle to you.' But this had little effect on the boy.

In 1855 he went to Bredasdorp as a clerk in his father's legal office. There matters went from bad to worse and they were few evil experiences which he had not plumbed to the very depths. He even reached the stage when he contemplated suicide. The one restraining force on his life was the prophecy of his saintly grandmother (who must have been gifted with second sight to make it of Stefanus) that ' He too will be an intercessor '.

In 1858 he was sent to his uncle's farm 'Remhoogte' in the district of Prince Albert to learn agriculture. He was fond of his uncle, who was as manly as he was Christian, and the boy began to think seriously about mending his ways. He even took to reading the Bible and engaging in prayer-meetings, but he felt all the while that this was not the product of trust in Christ but a mere display of self-righteousness. The agent who won him for the faith was Gideon Kotze, an Oudtshoorn teacher, who preached on the meaning of faith as absolute trust in an exalted Saviour. When Stefanus heard the teacher, he recognized that this man possessed an inner peace to which Stefanus was a stranger. This experience disturbed him profoundly. The following evening when it was his turn to attend to the distilling of the brandy under the stars he reviewed the Gadarene descent of his life. Early the next morning, when, after a short sleep, he resumed his duty, he cried out in an agony of frustration and despair, ' O Lord, what shall I do? I have tried everything and nothing helps. I can neither pray nor weep any longer. Be merciful to me.' His extremity proved God's opportunity, and he felt as truly as St. Augustine in the Milan garden or Martin Luther in the Erfurt monastery, that the abandonment of self in the trust of Christ relieves the tensions and bitternesses

10

of life. His heart, like theirs, was flooded with the assurance of God's unchanging love for him in Christ Jesus.

Immediately after this vivid experience of the dark night of the soul and of being ' translated from the Kingdom of darkness into the Kingdom of the love of God's dear Son ', he vowed to become a missionary to the heathen. He wrote offering his services to the Missionary Committee of the Dutch Reformed Church in the Cape. This letter crossed one sent to him by his future father-in-law, Ds. Neethling, the Chairman of this Commission, asking if he was prepared to come to Stellenbosch to prepare for a missionary vocation. This coincidence he interpreted as Divine approval for his plan.

After completing his training he went to Fransch Hoek to act as *locum tenens* for Ds. Ham. Here he was greatly beloved both by the Europeans and the Coloured. They were exceedingly sorry to see him go, although his stay had only been a short one, but they bowed to his inalterable determination to be a missionary. They presented him with food and equipment for his travels and one friend gave him a complete set of harness for his oxen. He wrote to the latter: ' The *riempies* shall be the prayers of the people of Fransch Hoek to tie the heathen to the throne of God.'

His farewell service and commissioning as a missionary took place at Stellenbosch and was conducted jointly by Di. Andrew Murray and J. H. Neethling. It was indicated that his sphere of service would be the Zoutpansberg as assistant to Ds. Mackidd.

Hitherto little progress had been made by the D.R.C. in missions. In 1857 a Missionary Committee had been set up but there were no candidates until Dr. Robertson of Stellenbosch brought back with him Henry Gonin of Switzerland and Mackidd of Scotland. The former was sent to begin work at Saulspoort and the latter in the Zoutpansberg, where he preached to a motley series of

congregations consisting of the Makapan and Gwamba
Natives and the Coloured descendants of Conrad Buys
(whose fascinating story has been retold by Sarah Ger-
trude Millin in *King of the Bastards*).   Thus, the ordination of the first Afrikaans-speaking South African born
missionary was a red-letter day in the calendar of the
Dutch Reformed Church.   Mackidd had lost his wife by
death and Hofmeyr came in response to his SOS to the
Missionary Committee.

Accompanied only by a Coloured man, Jan Zerf,
Hofmeyr took the long lonely road to the Zoutpansberg
from the Cape.   He travelled through Bain's Kloof, Ceres,
Prince Albert, Beaufort West, Murraysburg, Richmond,
Hanover and Colesberg.   In the Free State he passed
through Philippolis, Bloemfontein and Kroonstad, where he
was asked to hold a service in the Landdrost's office where
he met Sarel Cilliers.   He continued his journey through
Potchefstroom and Pretoria, being welcomed by Ds. Mackidd in the Zoutpansberg on 4 February 1865. Immediately
he took lessons in Sechuana from Mackidd.   He says that
when he arrived he found neither a baptized Native nor
any African Christian officer in the Church (whether
pastor, evangelist, teacher or catechist).   In this sea of
paganism Mackidd was the only Christian island, and the
unsuccessful struggle for converts was taking its toll of
him.   Indeed, after his wife's death Mackidd had no longer
any wish to live.   Within a few months both the missionaries were prostrate with malaria.   Hofmeyr recovered
but Mackidd died, leaving the assistant in full charge of
the station only a few months after his arrival.   This was
the situation to try a man of faith, and Hofmeyr emerged
victorious from it despite sickness and danger from the
guerilla warfare between the burghers and the neighbouring Native clans.   Indeed, this war ravaged his station
and he had to build it anew from the ground up.   It was
truly a baptism of fire for the missionary.

In April 1866 he went back to Stellenbosch and after
six months of further theological studies he was ordained
a missionary at Wynberg. He returned to *Goedgedacht*,
the mission station, with a wife (Ds. Neethling's sister
and a tower of strength) and an assistant, Pieter Dempers.

On a pioneer mission station great patience is required
for the results are slow in coming. The first considerable
success was achieved among the Buys clan who experienced a great religious revival at *Goedverwacht* (their
home) in 1876. A most unusual feature of this revival
was that it began in the children's prayer-meeting. Praying
and singing went on all through the nights for many days.
But to those who might be inclined to criticize it as mere
emotionalism, it could be reported that fifty-five years
after the event many of the children of the revival were
pillars of the Church and not a few had spent their lives
as evangelists among the Banyai people. Hofmeyr was
himself the child of a religious revival and he believed
that his own experience might be repeated by his charges.
In 1877 there was a second revival and in fourteen days
as many as fifty persons were converted, including an old
witch. Mackidd saw no fruit of his sowing, but by 1877
the faith of Stefanus Hofmeyr had been so remarkably
rewarded that he had a baptized community of over 700
Christians around him. The same power of the Spirit was
evident in his preaching among the European farmers and
their families in the Zoutpansberg.

Hofmeyr was the founder of the congregations of
Louis Trichardt, Pietersburg, Soekmekaar and the Lowveld.
He laboured among them for sixteen years, visiting
them once every three months to celebrate the *Nagmaal*
with them. Some of them were contemptuous of him
at first as the ' Kaffir-minister '. Some even attended his
services as spies and spread slanderous rumours about his
activities; but he was blessed with a spirit which was invincible because he had no room for bitterness in his soul.

What he must have required in the way of a forgiving heart can be imagined from the following incident recorded in his famous book *Twintig Jaren in de Zoutpansbergen*:

> A certain farmer who later became my deacon was at first hostile towards me and it seemed as if he really wanted to knock me about. In the little town of Schoemansdal I was always a stranger. I had to outspan on the market-square where I had to eat, sleep and conduct worship, for it seemed as if no one would have me in his house. But later, when General (now President) Kruger paid a visit to Schoemansdal he asked me to conduct Divine service. The Lord had heard my prayer and this strengthened my faith. . . .

Not all Afrikaners were hostile at first, for Hofmeyr writes:

> And what can I say of a man like Andries Duvenage, who insisted on offering us his huge house, half of his garden and lands for our own use as long as we wanted to stay on his farm and who also, whenever his wife baked, sent us bread and helped us in so many different ways?

In time he became so beloved by his white charges that when there was a projected union of the D.R.C. and the *Hervormde Kerk* congregations in the Zoutpansberg in 1885, he was invited to became minister of the church. When he declined because of his primary missionary responsibility, they invited him to act as consulent until they could find a minister of their own.

A welcome interruption in his duties was twice made by the official visits of his brother-in-law as Secretary of the Missionary Committee. On the first occasion Ds. Neethling was greatly moved by the visit of a blind old Christian Native from Malietseland. He was the only Christian in a pagan neighbourhood and had braved a lion-infested country to put his question to the missionary: ' *Monite Mogolo*, when are you going to send us a minister?'

Needless to say, the necessary assurance was given, for Hofmeyr had made a point of training Native evangelists as the shock-troops of the Gospel in surrounding Native heathendom. In fact, Hofmeyr was a pioneer of the missionary method of decentralization. Other missionaries had gathered their converts around them in a ' Christian colony ' on the mission station, but it was Hofmeyr's far-sighted policy to urge the Christian Natives to return to their kraals and make their Christian witness there, with the occasional encouragement of evangelists to keep them in touch with the mission station.

Though he did not himself go to Banyailand (the earlier name for Mashonaland), he was in a real sense the pioneer missionary in that country through the many evangelists he trained to preach the Gospel in that land. That work is to-day focused in the splendid missionary tradition of *Morgenster*. Indeed, in 1866 he offered to go as a missionary to Banyailand if a substitute could be found for him at *Goedgedacht*, but none was available.

He was also a true friend of the Paris Evangelical Missionary Society, as of the Swiss mission in the Transvaal. He persuaded the Paris Society to work in the present Southern Rhodesia and was most helpful in the advice and facilities of guides he gave to François Coillard on his trek to the Zambezi. The latter said of Hofmeyr: ' He is a true Afrikaner, a man mighty in faith and works, his heart burning with love and zeal in the service of his Lord.' This is a testimony, like Moffat's, of one great missionary to another. He could not bear to think of the degradation and fear in which the heathen lived and sent evangelists whom he could hardly spare for his own wide work into Banyailand, one of whom, Gabriel Buys, was murdered by the Mashona.

This lonely pioneer gave his entire life to the folk in the far-off Zoutpansberg. His closing years were lived in much heroism amid suffering. He suffered from erysipelas

and neuralgia, chest and heart trouble. Sometimes it
seemed as if his whole frame was writhing in pain. He
had two rondavels built on an elevated place above the
mission station, which he called his ' Patmos '. The pain
he felt in his head made it impossible for him to conduct
services and he found he could only with difficulty attend
part of a service in his latter days. The hearty singing of
the Africans made his head buzz and hence he listened only
to the sermon. In these days his great help was his son-in-
law, Ds. J. W. Daneel, who relieved him of much responsibility. Nevertheless, he refused to be idle and he visited,
prayed and read the Bible to the sick and the blind on
the station until the very last. He died on 9 July 1905.
Only the day before he had said, in reference to his
daughter's burial, ' Bury her where you think fit, but I
want to be buried among my own people '. He was
therefore buried with the Africans to whom he had given
his life.

He was a modest man and our best estimates of his
importance and influence are obtained from those who
knew him intimately and studied his life. A number of
these have been collected by Ds. J. W. L. Hofmeyr in
his book, *Die Lewe van Stefanus Hofmeyr*. That this
man was a saint we learn from one of his own evangelists
who said:

> You never know when *Meneer* will be sleeping. Whenever
> you look out you see his candle burning. And if I am
> sleeping underneath the wagon I hear *Meneer* reading and
> praying long before the dawn. He prays for many men and
> places of which we have no knowledge. We hear him praying
> for Uganda but we do not know where that place is. . . .

It is said that no man is a hero to his own valet, but
Hofmeyr was a saint to his own evangelist!

He was not only a great man of prayer, but an inde-
fatigable evangelist. Surely no man ever had an equal
concern to win every uncommitted soul he met for Christ.

One conversation he had is typical of the man's unflagging zeal. Once when he was out riding he met a fellow-European, unknown to him, and the following dialogue took place.

Stranger: 'Good day, cousin.'

S.H.:   'Good day, my friend.'

Stranger: 'It is h----- hot!'

S.H.:   'I know a hotter place.'

Stranger: 'Then it must be h----- warm there!'

S.H.:   'I can well believe that!'

They then outspanned and Hofmeyr took out his small Bible and lay on the grass reading it.

Stranger: 'What is that book you are reading?'

S.H.:   'The instructions of my Father.'

Stranger: 'But why do you speak so quaintly? I merely asked you what you were reading.'

S.H.:   'I tell you truly that these are the instructions my Father. In other words, a Bible.'

Stranger: 'Are you by any chance a minister?'

S.H.:   'No, I'm not a minister.'

Stranger: 'What are you then?'

S.H.:   'I am only the old missionary, Hofmeyr. See, my custom is whenever I meet someone to pray with him. Come, let us pray together.'

They knelt down together, but as soon as Mnr. Hofmeyr opened his eyes the man was out of sight!

The missionary enthusiasm of this pioneer of the Spirit is expressed movingly in a letter he sent to Major Malan, a retired officer of the French army and missionary:

Our heart is full of joy whenever by faith we can see the footprints of the king of kings. For with Him to fight and to conquer are one and the same. It is he who can truly save. *Veni, vidi, vici.* . . . O, how I long to tell the heathen that we can conquer without guns! Up to this point our might has been exercised by fire-arms, but we shall not yet go into our winter quarters. O, that we all and every missionary in the whole world were spiritual warriors feeling that each one of us is but a part of the whole army. How quickly we would then bring the heathen to the foot of the Saviour!

It seemed to Hofmeyr as if his whole life would never compensate his Lord for the cruel injustice done Him on the Cross. Like the first great missionary, St. Paul, he could say, 'For the love of Christ constraineth me.'

The faith of Stefanus Hofmeyr was like the mustard seed of the parable which became a great tree. Only twenty-five years after his death in 1905 the missionary work of the Dutch Reformed Church of the Cape Province had so expanded that it could boast of approximately 20,000 members, 12,000 catechumens and 60,000 children in the schools of the mission. This was the result of the work of a man who was the friend equally of the whites, the coloured and the blacks for Christ's sake. No greater tribute than this could be paid to any South African.

CHAPTER XVII

ERNEST CREUX AND PAUL BERTHOUD

F^{OR} two young men to discover a tribe, reduce its
language to writing, evangelize it and build up a
strong Church within it, and still be alive to celebrate
the jubilee of the mission is a remarkable achievement.
This is exactly what Creux and Berthoud did. Their importance is threefold: they are brilliant examples of missionary perseverance, despite the most crushing blows;
they show the missionary's essential role as reconciler; they
prove the compulsion of the love of Christ to be the
most dynamic force in history — by laying down their
Swiss bones in Southern Africa in the territory where they
had poured out their lives and lost many of their beloved
children. They are the founders and consolidators of a
Mission which boasts to-day among the Thonga-speaking
peoples of the northern Transvaal a Christian community
of over 5,000 souls and 132 places of worship, and among
the Ronga-speaking people of Mozambique a Christian
community of over 12,000 souls and 166 places of worship.
It is, moreover, the Swiss mission which has conspicuously
devoted itself to the task of shepherding the lepers, the
prisoners, and the insane, for Christ's sake. For this they
are honoured not only by Christians, but by philanthropists and humanists who salute such altruistic service of
humanity.

These two different and complementary servants of
Christ seem to have attracted each other as opposites in
their days as theological students. According to their biographer, H. A. Junod, Creux was impulsive and poetic, a
great pastor and lover of souls, while Berthoud was the

reflective scientist and organiser. They shared a dream
for the Free Church of the Canton of Vaud in Switzerland
and for themselves. They wished the Church to form its
own missionary society and to accept them as its pioneer
missionaries.

Creux was attracted to the missionary calling by the
influence of a saintly pastor, Louis Bridel, who was a
great missionary enthusiast in Lausanne and neighbourhood, and, although he lived beside a charming mill on
the banks of the Flon, spread with orchards beneath the
vast overshadowing mountains, he dreamed incessantly
of dusky pagans beneath a torrid sky.

Berthoud's chief spiritual influence was his own saintly
father, the Rev. Henri Berthoud of Morges in the
Vaudois Canton. Of his seven sons, two became missionaries in South Africa, one a minister, and a fourth a theological professor. Paul Berthoud first thought of missions
when his father performed the marriage service of Germond, who went out as a missionary to Basutoland under
the Paris Evangelical Missionary Society, and declared at
the reception afterwards, ' It will be the happiest day of
my life when one of my sons leaves for missionary service '.
On a later occasion, Paul's father heard his son's penetrating voice when he was playing with some companions
in a railed-in space in the town. The pastor put his
lips to the railings and called out: ' You there! You,
with the voice of a Stentor! You'll make a fine missionary in the Indies. You'll be able to preach to the crowds
from a ship and be heard, like the Lord himself!'

The two friends wrote to the supreme court of their
Church once their course was completed, pleading to be
sent as missionaries. It was several years before their
dream was realized. They were, however, permitted to
join their fellow-countrymen Mabille and Germond who
were in Basutoland, until such time as their Church should
found its own society. First, however, they had to under-

go further training in Europe before their missionary apprenticeship in Basutoland. They were sent to the University of Edinburgh to learn English and the rudiments of medicine; Creux being impatient, soon left, whilst Berthoud gained a more thorough medical training. Creux spent a good deal of the time as a chaplain to Protestant prisoners in Bavaria, during the Franco-German War. He also married an English lady, Miss Matilda Ansell, who was to be his devoted companion for fifty-seven years. Berthoud married a Miss Exchaquet, a fellow-patriot.

In February, 1872, Creux and his wife embarked in the *Norseman* for South Africa. They had little opinion of the accommodation or their fellow-passengers. Creux wrote: ' I don't know how we shall live in these boxes for thirty-eight days; the smell is as unpleasant as a hospital; a doubtful light flickers from an opening no bigger than the bottom of my hat. We are crowded with passengers, nearly all of them diamond-seekers. The company is not very congenial.' The voyage took only twenty-eight days and before long they were landing at Port Elizabeth and trekking on towards Basutoland. At Aliwal North they met Adolphe Mabille, the greatest friend and counsellor the Swiss mission had in its early days.

Nine months after Creux, Berthoud and his wife left Switzerland for ' Switzerland-in-South-Africa '. Evantually they shared the Creux home in Morija. Here they acquired a Bantu language, Sotho, habituated themselves to the climate and ways of South Africa, and were taught missionary strategy by a brilliant exponent, Mabille.

In 1873 it was decided that a prospecting expedition should go to the north, led by Mabille, who was to take Native catechists and Paul Berthoud as his chief assistant. Berthoud's comments on Pretoria make interesting reading, over seventy-five years later. He wrote: ' Pretoria is like all the other towns of this country; white or gray villas built of rough bricks; flowerless gardens, fruit-trees, eucalyptus and willow-trees; a few shops, which have everything and more — except the very thing you want; grass or dust provides the street surface where horses, oxen, dogs, goats, sheep and antelopes walk about freely. Some young Englishmen and Boers stared at us as if we had dropped out of the sky!' Their destinaiton was the Bapedi people, but the chief resisted their appeals. They continued their northern trek until they reached the magnificent Zoutpansberg. There they were welcomed by a Dutch missionary, Hofmeyr, whose elders thought little of their missionary's suggestion that the newcomers should settle among the Gwamba in the Spelonken district. These people were known as the *Knobneusen* (knobbly-nosed, because of their curious nasal tattooing) by the Boers. Hofmeyr's elders alleged: 'They are thieves, liars, tricksters, and, apart from this, they speak a very difficult tongue. We don't think it is even possible to understand it.' Mabille made the perfect retort: 'These are just the kind of people we are looking for. Didn't Jesus come to seek and to save the lost?'

The Spelonken area was then settled as the field of the Vaudois mission, and, leaving two Sotho catechists in possession of the field, the expedition hurried back to Basutoland to report.

In 1875 Creux, Berthoud, their families and Native assistants started out for their new home. It must have been a curious sight, their caravan of thirty-nine persons (including two young babies) and over a hundred beasts (horses, cattle, sheep and goats). On 9 July 1875, they reached the Spelonken district, as their caravan descended on to the mountain-encircled plain, reminding them of their own beloved Switzerland. They named the new station Valdézia.

The living-quarters were primitive, consisting of a rude farmhouse and tumbledown shop which they had purchased from a Scots settler, named Watt. The Creux family divided the shop into three sections and made that their abode. The Berthouds lived in three conical huts, in windowless darkness and damp.

The dream of the theological students had become a reality. But their first joy in bringing the Christian Gospel to pagans was soon overshadowed by two serious setbacks. The dream, indeed, was followed by two terrifying nightmares. In their second year, the two men were taken into protective custody by the order of the Transvaal Government and the infant mission was leaderless for several anxious months, during which their wives saw the battle between the Boers and a rebellious Bapedi tribe on the very doorstep of the mission. The missionaries supposed that the Boers either suspected them of sympathy with the Bapedi or wanted them out of the way during the punitive expedition in their neighbourhood.

The returned missionaries were cheered by a visit from the redoubtable French missionary, François Coillard, in 1877, who saw the first fruits of the Harvest of the Holy Spirit, in the baptism of seventeen converts. The mission suffered a more terrible blow in 1879 and 1880, when it was struck down by malaria. The climate, the poor accommodation, and overwork had weakened the resistance of both families to this fever. Mme Berthoud died and her husband had the harrowing experience of watching every one of his five children follow their mother to the grave. This broke his heart and crushed his faith. Not long afterwards three of Creux's children died from diphtheria. The seed of the Gospel among the Thonga-speaking people was indeed fertilized with the blood of sacrifice.

Even these anguished experiences were turned to gain in the providence of God, for they spurred the parent Society to greater efforts. The Free Churches of Neu-châtel and Geneva joined the Vaudois in the enterprise in

South Africa and thus formed the Swiss mission. Paul's brother, Henri Berthoud, came out as a reinforcement of the ranks. And, most significant of all, a Native assistant, Josepha, reported that there were hundreds of the Gwamba tribe in Portuguese territory, thus increasing the potential harvest. In 1880 he was set apart as an evangelist. Thus, in five years the new Church had itself undertaken missionary work!

Berthoud returned to Switzerland to recuperate physically and spiritually. He also saw to the printing of the first literary fruit of the missionaries in the indigenous language. It was the famous *Boukou*, a Christian manual, which included the first chapters of Genesis, the Ten Commandments, a Harmony of the Gospels and fifty-seven hymns.

Meantime Creux was proving the greatness of a forgiving spirit. Although he had been wrongfully imprisoned by the Transvaal Government, he willingly came to its aid, as a peace-maker between the *veldkornet* Joubert and Makhatu (chief or the Bavenda). Joubert was leading a punitive expedition against the Bavenda who refused to pay their taxes. On this occasion Creux took his life in his hands in approaching the hideout of the chief, but he established himself as the friend of both contestants. Incidentally, if his mission had failed, the Bavenda would probably have been decimated and he a corpse.

On Paul Berthoud's return from Switzerland with Ruth Junod (his second wife), he took charge of the medical work with great devotion. Occasionally, his operations were attempts to correct the ugly failure of a medicine-man. Once, for instance, he had to remove part of a woman's jawbone through her cheek, which had been left embedded there by a Native sawbones. When Berthoud eventually dislodged this bone, the reluctant tooth, which had not yielded to the Native ' dentist ', was still in the bone!

Berthoud's finest work was, however, done in Mozambique. He volunteered (as did Creux) to remain there as soon as he heard that a new chief of the Gwamba in Portuguese territory was persecuting the Christians. The first station of the Coastal mission was established at Rikhatla in 1886, and here the Berthouds lived until 1888 when they transferred to the more strategic post of Lourenço Marques. In those days this city was known as the white man's grave, medically and morally. The Swiss mission justly claims the honour of being the first Protestant society to operate in Portuguese East Africa. Berthoud's organizing genius found full scope in erecting buildings, in supervising African congregations, and in exercising a firm but fair discipline. He was, also, an excellent Ronga linguist. Within seven years he had established four stations and gathered a community of 1,000 adults and 200 children. His success may largely be attributed to his firm conviction that the future of missions in Africa lay in the thorough training of African evangelists. His best helper throughout was Pastor Calvin Mapopé, whose brother was ordained a minister by Creux and served with equal distinction in the northern Transvaal.

Meanwhile Creux's work at Elim was going through a very trying phase. The Christian Natives seemed to be reverting to paganism. Gold had been found on the Reef in 1886 and the Africans flocked to the city of gold, returning with white money and white vices. They despised the kinsmen who remained with the tribe and derided Native teachers and catechists as ' mere missionary employees at five shillings per week!' A wave of covetousness and intemperance seemed to overthrow the very standards which the mission had established at such great cost. Even the schoolchildren showed their contempt by playing truant *en masse*.

In 1896 there was another great time of testing. Drought, locusts, famine, cattle-disease and dysentery followed hard upon each other's deadly heels. But the perseverance of the missionaries was equal to the task. Once again, man's extremity proved God's opportunity. Out of the depths of their misery the Gwambas recognized their infidelity and cried to God. The tide of unbelief turned in 1897, coinciding with the arrival of Dr. Liengme, skilled director of souls and physician. Several conversions and returns to grace reached a climax in the submission of the chief of the tribe to God. 'He has conquered me', said the chief.

By the turn of the century both mission fields were firmly established with Creux as Director in Pretoria and Berthoud as Director in Lourenço Marques. Berthoud's cup of suffering had again to be drunk to the dregs, for his wife died of dysentery, as did three others in the missionary family. Undefeated in spirit, though greatly enfeebled in body, he crowned his task by erecting a vast church in Lourenço Marques, with seating accommodation for 1,200. He lived on as the Grand Old Man of Missions and was greatly beloved by his own staff and the Anglican and Methodist missionaries. Writing, translating and astronomy were his hobbies in the latter days of his life.

Creux's ministry in Pretoria was being extended in three entirely new directions. He was ministering to lepers, to prisoners and to the insane. Like his Lord, his outstretched arms welcomed the outcast and dejected, the repugnant and the forgotten. However unattractive the bodily casket, this Christian Greatheart sought zealously for the jewel of the soul that lay within Everyman. He wrote of the lepers (is there any more self-denying Christian task than caring for them?): ' I see in front of me all that can be described as the most hideous, physically, but Jesus loves them, we love them in His love, and,

11

in return, their poor suffering hearts are filled with love and gratitude.' This sense of entering into the sufferings of Christ, the authentic Christian note, has been superbly expressed in the Chapel in the Leper Colony, a few miles out of Pretoria, in Sir Frank Brangwyn's murals depicting the Stations of the Cross. This, incidentally, is one of the art treasures of Africa and little known.

Creux's great pastoral gift was also seen in his deep concern for prisoners. In a matter of twenty years it was his unenviable task to bring peace to the souls of 400 Africans in the condemned cells in Pretoria gaol. What could a minister of God say to men over whom the shadow of the scaffold hung? He brought them (many of them hardened criminals) to a sense of penitence, declared the forgiving love of God in Christ, described the eternal life beyond the reach of the rope, and retold movingly the story of the Prodigal Son and the pardoned criminal on his lesser cross at Calvary. He surely had his reward in heaven?

The two lifelong missionary comrades were alive, though hardly well, to celebrate the Golden Jubilee of the foundation of the mission in 1925. They were overjoyed to learn of the rapturous appreciation of the Swiss who filled the Cathedral of Lausanne and the great Hall of the Reformation in Geneva to give God and His servants honour. At Valdézia there was a vast throng of 3,000 people to celebrate the triumphs of Christ in Africa.

Ernest Creux died in 1929 and was buried in Pretoria; nine months later Paul Berthoud followed his comrade.

The invincible faith in an invincible God, the deep love of Africans for Christ's sake, and the creative forgiveness of their relationships with all men, scintillate more brightly in the twilight of our after-age.

CHAPTER XVIII

MOTHER CECILE

TWO great cathedrals are being slowly raised to the glory of God in the Church of England, one the design of Edward Maufe in Guildford, the other the work of Sir Giles Gilbert Scott in Liverpool. Scott was only twenty-one years old when his designs for the latter cathedral were accepted and he lived to see the Lady-chapel completed, with its long but slender pillars pointing like the hands of a saint uplifted in prayer. In one of its stained-glass windows the work of a great and devout woman is commemorated, as a representative of the religious life. The woman depicted there is Mother Cecile, the foundress of the Community of the Resurrection of Our Lord. This, in itself, indicates the pre-eminence of this devout servant of Christ in South Africa.

Equally remarkable is the fact that a girl of twenty-one should have been the first member of this new religious order for women within the Anglican Communion, and that the wide and varied activities of this community should have been established on firm foundations by her in the twenty-two years between her arrival in the Cape Colony and her death at the age of forty-three.

Her memorial is, in fact, the Community of the Resurrection, and the tribute to Mother Cecile and her successors can only be paid by the teachers and members of the Church of the Province, the orphans and destitute children, and the pupils of many races, who were her spiritual family. True to its title, the Community of the Resurrection gave a new and living hope in Christ to thousands of underprivileged South Africans of all races, and through

its renowned Training College in Grahamstown it has
given its teachers in training a sense, not merely of the
privilege of this profession, but of the need for the consecration of their talents to the service of the Teacher of
teachers.   In saluting Mother Cecile, therefore, we celebrate first the Incarnate Son of God Who was her constant inspiration, and we remember the faithful, anonymous (and often unthanked) devotion of the handmaids
of Our Lord, known collectively as the Community of the
Resurrection.

What a mistake it is to regard religious Sisters as those
who have retired from the pain, the struggle, the weari-
ness, and the tears of the world!   Their life of discipline
and of service for Christ's sake has equipped them to
serve Our Lord and His needier children with more con-
centration of purpose.   They have severed their human
ties of kinship, to serve the supernatural family of Christ.
A mere catalogue of the work they undertake will disabuse
any reader who wrongly believes that they are cloistered,
self-congratulating souls.

Their activities which radiate from the Mother House
in Grahamstown (the beating heart of which is the
chapel) extend through the Diocese of Grahamstown, to
the Transvaal, to Southern Rhodesia and even to Northern
Rhodesia.   They undertake parochial, missionary, educational and social work.   Within the limits of this essay
only a few examples may be selected.   In Grahamstown
they have one of the finest residential training colleges
for European women teachers in Southern Africa and an
orphanage accommodating over a hundred children.   In
Port Elizabeth, St. Mark's Mission School caters for the
needs of over five hundred Coloured children, whilst the
St. Francis Xavier Mission is concerned with the spiritual
needs of the Chinese in the same city.   The Sisters are
also represented in East London and Queenstown.

At Grace Dieu, near Pietersburg, the community is responsible for staffing the boarding hostels and the industrial training of the African girls who attend the Diocesan Training College. They also run a hostel in Rosettenville.

In Southern Rhodesia they are well represented in Salisbury, Bulawayo, in St. Faith's Mission, Rusape, and in St. Monica's Mission House which they manage in conjunction with the notable St. Augustine's Mission at Penhalonga. In this diocese they undertake boarding, orphanage, teaching and industrial training responsibilities.

All this work is the fruit of the seed planted by Mother Cecile, who must be acclaimed one of the most outstanding women missionaries in the whole continent of Africa.

According to G. K. Chesterton, ' Religion makes the ordinary man extraordinary.' In the case of that gifted woman, Annie Cecilia Isherwood, her talents were used to ensure a supernatural success. Her 'success story' records the success of consecration and obedience to the Heavenly Vision not the vulgar and trivial success of personal ambition.

She was born into a cultured and comfortable English home in 1862, the daughter of Captain and Mrs. Isherwood of Hillingdon Lodge, Uxbridge. Among her ancestors on the distaff side was one Ramsbottom who signed *Magna Charta* and another who represented the Royal Borough of Windsor in Parliament. The happiness of her home life was rudely disturbed by the death of her mother when Cecilia was only eight. The second tragedy, the death of her father five years later, completely broke up the home. It can only be imagined how deeply so affectionate and sensitive a child was bereaved by the loss of both her parents. But, in the Divine mercy, she was being prepared to understand and help the motherless and the orphaned, out of her own heart-rending experience. Thus God cuts the threads of the tapestry of life and later reties them in compassionate patterns.

Inevitably, the background of her life was unsettled in these years, whether she lived with her elder brother in Brighton, or, as later, with her father's friends, General Sir James and Lady Browne, who adopted her almost as a daughter. But she found the anchor of faith in St. Peter's Church, Eaton Square. On a sombre winter afternoon, the light streaming through its many-coloured windows invited her inside. On this occasion the address of the Rector (the Rev. G. H. Wilkinson) seemed for her ears alone, and she decided to ask to be confirmed. The real turning-point in her life was the systematic and loving instruction in the Christian doctrine and way of life given by the Rector, who was later to become the Primus, the leader of the Bishops of the Anglican Church in Scotland. The only spiritual influence on her life at all comparable was the advice and sympathy of Bishop Webb of Grahamstown, who was the inspirer and counsellor of the Community of the Resurrection in his see.

After her confirmation, she devoted herself heart and soul to parochial work, and responded unconditionally to Bishop Webb's suggestion that she devote her life to working in the diocese of Grahamstown. So complete was her sense of dedication, that she asked the Bishop to set her apart as a deaconess. Thus it was that, in 1883, she was one of the party of workers which the new Bishop brought from England to assist him in the diocese.

She plunged into the work immediately on her arrival, and no task was too humble to be undertaken. Already her deep sense of social justice and ardent sympathy for the downtrodden were manifest. Within a few months she was alarmed by the condition of the Cape prisons, finding that old and new offenders, adults and children were herded together indiscriminately. Waifs and strays, in the absence of any orphanages and reformatories, were also housed in the prisons. Deaconess Cecile therefore spent several days in Cape Town urging the case for a reform of prisons on the members of the legislature as they entered or left the parliamentary lobbies. Directly as a result of this twenty-one-year-old petitioner's pleas, improvements were made, after a commission had investigated. Moreover, she made her own practical contribution to the solution of the problem by founding an orphanage in Grahamstown, and by the initiation of a Home for Unmarried Mothers in Port Elizabeth. This constructive work, it must be repeated, was begun by a newcomer to the country, a girl in years, but a woman in maturity and decisiveness.

It is not surprising that Bishop Webb asked her if she would consent to be the first member of a women's religious community, to be named the Community of the Resurrection of Our Lord, the second Anglican Sisterhood to be founded in South Africa. She gladly responded, as no one was more convinced that a life of devotion to others for Christ's sake could only be lived as the outcome of prayer and spiritual discipline. Bishop Webb received her as a Novice in Bishopsbourne Chapel in 1884, and she was professed by him on her twenty-fifth birthday in 1887. She lived in the presence of her Risen Lord and her character radiated the joyous sacrifice of her Master. Her favourite counsel to the other Sisters in time of difficulty was, ' We must use our knees '. They averred that long before the others were down in the mornings, she would be in the Chapel pleading for the other Sisters and for the work. Her joyousness was catching.

The early years of the community were marked by great poverty. An attractive property named Eden Grove in the neighbourhood of the Botanical Gardens of Grahamstown, was purchased as the home of the community, but the payment of mortgage forced the Sisters to live at a bare subsistence level. Mother Cecile and the Sisters were often reduced to the pathetic shifts of penury. For example, if the weather was bad and the roads muddy, there was only one cloak and one pair of stout shoes between them all. Similarly, at one stage, they could afford to use only one lamp, which was carried from the refectory to the chapel, and thence to the dormitory corridor. Like the primitive spiritual Communism of the *Acts of the Apostles*, they ' had all things in common ' and ' all that believed were of one heart and mind '. The turning-point was marked by the gift of five shillings from a Native priest, who insisted that his donation was for ' the ladies with their heads tied up '. When the gift was almost refused on the score that the Sisters were doing nothing for Africans, the priest answered, ' But you will!' How prophetic was his faith that the compassion of the Sisters could not be confined to the channels of one race!

If these were days of penury and struggle, they were also days of adventure and danger. The Port Elizabeth Sisters could have told of many cases of ingratitude and even spite on the part of parents whose uncared-for children had been rescued by the Sisters. But the Sisters did not complain for they remembered the unparalleled sacrifice of their Lord on His Cross.

Moreover, who would wish to complain when Mother Cecile herself took more than her fair share of hazards? Once when she was travelling to the Herschel Mission, their post-cart was caught in a terrifying thunderstorm. An ox was struck dead by lightning a few yards in front of them. The Native driver was petrified with fear, and unable to move an inch forward. The Reverend Mother took the reins in her own hands and, by sheer determination, drove against wind and rain.

On another occasion she was in jeopardy whilst rescuing a European child from the Malays in Port Elizabeth. The child's mother had sold the baby to the Malays, and, on her deathbed, pleaded with Mother Cecile to recover the child. Mother Cecile had an order from the magis-

trate and was attended by a policeman in the background.
They walked to the Malay quarters and the house in which
the child was living was surrounded by a sullen group
of Malays.   Mother Cecile, catching a glimpse of the baby,
ducked in under the throng, seized the child, folded her
in the wide sleeves of her habit, and ran off.   The
menacing Malays followed her the whole of the way to
the station.   She was safe from attack only when the
train left the station.

Of compassion and courage the Reverend Mother had
God's plenty.   She was also a remarkable planner and
administrator.   Schools, orphanages, homes, hostels were
erected and staffed through her enthusiasm and drive.
She urged, for one example, the provincial authorities to
establish a children's ward in the hospital in Port Elizabeth,
and this was actually staffed by the Sisters of the community until 1898.   Her greatest achievement, however,
was the Training College in Grahamstown.   She planned
it and raised most of the funds for it and arranged with
Dr. Muir, the Superintendent-General of Education for
the Cape, for it to receive state assistance.   This great
task was undertaken when the first symptoms of her
fatal malady were apparent and when she was often in
great pain.

St. Peter's Higher Grade School was founded in 1885
and twelve years later it was recognized as a training
college for teachers.   It was, of course, too small for the
needs of teachers in training in the Eastern Province, and
was, moreover, a church training college.   Mother
Cecile's problem was how to secure government recognition
and financial assistance for a denominational institution.
How, in fact, could the college be broadened to welcome
intending teachers from many communions (and thus
secure the government grant) and yet not lose its own
distinctive ecclesiastical heritage?   Her ability and Dr.
Muir's admiration for her personality appear to have won

the day. Her strategy was brilliant. It was founded on three principles: firstly, it was definitely to remain a work of the Community of the Resurrection who were to provide the funds for the new buildings, but for part only of the new salaries; secondly, an attempt would be made to welcome girls of both English and Dutch stock and make them feel thoroughly at home in the college; thirdly, ministers of the non-Anglican communions were given the right of entry to instruct pupils of their own allegiance in the faith and order of their churches.

The stone-laying ceremony of the new training college in 1904, at which both Bishop Wilkinson (her old Rector in the Eaton Square days) and Canon Scott Holland were present, represented a triumph for the Reverend Mother's planning and enthusiasm, not to mention her powers of fund-raising. The many daughters of this institution throughout Southern Africa and overseas have good cause to rise up and call her blessed.

All the more blessed, indeed, in that the work was planned in the midst of deep suffering. In 1905 the pain was so constant that her medical adviser insisted on her returning to England for specialist treatment. She was, alas, beyond the aid of any human specialist, and she died in 1906 after bravely facing what she knew was a critical operation. The Archbishop of Canterbury and Bishop Wilkinson were present to officiate at the burial service and see the tired body of Mother Cecile committed to the earth in sure and certain hope of the Resurrection. They recognized that she had in twenty-three crowded years accomplished work that others as gifted might have taken many lives to complete.

What was the secret of her joy, her courage, her sacrifice and her compassion? In brief, it was the Incarnation, identification with and imitation of the Holy and Loving Son of God in His perfect Sacrifice on the Cross and in the faith and the promise of His glorious Resurrection. This was the source of her compassion for all the underprivileged. In her own words:

> We must never forget that Our Blessed Lord Himself first looked out in human form upon this world of ours in the face of a little child; and we want to nurture and train his children for Him, that their life and their work here on earth may be a steadfast looking up to the Face of Our Lord Jesus Christ.

The Crucifixion of the Incarnate Lord was also the dynamic of her endurance of privation and suffering. In her own beautiful phrasing:

> Nothing helps one so much as to fix one's mind on Christ and to let Him teach one how, from the Manger to the Cross, Incarnate Love gave to the uttermost. If we look long enough at that great fact, the nails may still be iron, but there comes the grace and strength not to wish to come down from our own cross.

Throughout we have used the title of ' Mother Cecile ' — ought we not rather to write of ' Saint Cecile '? The sparkle of this joyous saint is an inspiration and an example of the contribution that women make to the Church of God, even if few are as obedient as she was to the King and Head of the Church.

CHAPTER XIX

JOHN WHITE

A MAN is known by his friends, and John White was a magnet who drew diverse personalities to himself. One of them, whom he came to know only in the last years of suffering, was so impressed by the courage of the man that he wrote his biography. This was no less a personality than C. F. Andrews, the distinguished writer and missionary in India. His other friend and co-missionary was A. S. Cripps who identified himself so completely with the life of his charges that he has more claim than most to the often-distributed title of 'The twentieth-century St. Francis'. The poet-missionary Cripps and the preacher-missionary White are amongst the few in Southern Africa who have deserved the beatitude, 'Blessed are ye when men shall revile you, and persecute you, and say all manner of evil against you, falsely, for my sake, for great is your reward in Heaven'. They both endured taunts for their championship of the cause of the Mashona, and the greatly improved services (social and educational) for the African in Southern Rhodesia to-day are in no small measure the results of their persistent advocacy.

White's claim to fame is his extraordinary courage and compassion, his pioneering in the work of evangelism, the translation of the Scriptures, and in African education and citizenship. In him we salute an incorruptible Christian, and an outstanding example of the great outpouring of missionary devotion in Southern Rhodesia. Perhaps the characteristic which appeals most to our time in a missionary, apart from his constructive compassion for the unprivileged, was his whimsical sense of humour. He was a gay troubadour of Christ who demonstrated in himself the fulfilment of His Master's promise, ' I am come that they might have life and have it more abundantly '. There was nothing of the prig or the puritan in White: his goodness was winsome and winning.

Neither his birthplace nor his upbringing suggests the crucible of greatness. He was born in 1866, the eldest of a family of seven children in a remote farmhouse at Dearham in Cumberland, on the edge of the Lake District. His formal education was intermittent and consisted in childhood of the three R's taught in a widow's school. But his informal education was impressive and of incalculable benefit to him afterwards as a pioneer missionary. The open-air life developed a strong physique inherited from sturdy stock, and his experience of farming in Dearham and dairying at Workington (where the family removed later) gave him an insight into the independence of settlers in Southern Rhodesia, quite apart from its value for managing the agricultural side of missionary institutions. The Lakes and Fells are themselves an education in the appreciation of beauty. But what he valued most was the simple piety and love of his Methodist parents. Like many a boy brought up in a Christian home he took these things for granted, but, at the age of sixteen, he made his own far-reaching decision to serve Our Lord. It seems that a mission-preacher, the Rev. Thomas Waugh, visited Workington and appealed for conversions. Perhaps reticence held John White back, but his defences were down when a local preacher touched his arm and said quietly, ' Oh, John, won't you now at this very moment make your decision for Christ?' He replied, with equal simplicity, ' Yes, I will '.

A more sophisticated age that derides such experiences as emotional and ephemeral, and is as afraid of 'enthusiasm' as the most dignified eighteenth-century gentleman, is in danger of forgetting that it was by such directness that

Our Lord called the first disciples from their nets on the quayside. We need only record the fact that this decision stood the test of fifty-one hard years, and that by it a religion of ' the top of the mind ' was transformed into a religion of ' the bottom of the heart '. John White was, thereafter, Christ's willing bond-slave. If such wearing-the-heart-on-the-sleeve is the indispensable condition for fearlessness in God's service (' the perfect love that casteth out fear '), then let us have a surfeit of it! Conversely, some reticences are cowardice masquerading as courtesy.

In the ardour of his new allegiance John White wished to offer himself immediately for service as a lay-evangelist in Australia. His wise Superintendent Minister, recogniz-ing the gifts of the young man, urged him instead to go to a theological college and train as an ordained missionary and minister. White was admitted as a ministerial candi-date to Didsbury Wesleyan Methodist College in 1888. He was sent out by the British Conference to work in the Transvaal and it was during the last decade of the nine-teenth century when Jameson had penetrated into the land which to-day we know as Southern Rhodesia. John White was, in fact, filling a vacancy caused by the pros-pecting surveys of Watkins and Shimmin in Matebeleland and Mashonaland. In the charge given to him at his ordination, it was evident that he and his advisers expected that he would soon be pushing north. In retrospect the advice given him seems prophetic:

> Let him preserve his health so that he may use his body for the service and glory of God. Let him cultivate deep sym-pathy for the African races. Let him learn their languages. Let him, like the Great Exemplar Jesus Christ Our Lord, be a true man amongst his fellow-men.

He stayed impatiently for two years in the Transvaal, but even there he had a foretaste of the dangers that lay ahead of him. Once he was caught in the swirling currents of a river in spate, and had gone under twice, when he was rescued by the strong arms of a Dutch swimmer and friend.

At the end of April 1894, he left the Transvaal *en route* to Salisbury. It took the party seven days to reach the Limpopo River, and five days before they could cross it. Now they were in country infested by hyenas and lions. On one occasion, as they were preparing to halt, they heard the sudden, interrupted yelp of a dog. The grass was now over shoulder-height, so they kindled a fire and slept. At sunrise they trekked on, White leading the way. To continue in his own words:

We had tramped about four miles when suddenly, without warning, a large lion bounded out of the grass and stood on the path about six yards in front of me. It looked at me, and then, with two more big leaps, it was standing on a boulder about twenty yards away. There it stood looking at us. Keeping my eyes on the beast I walked backwards and got my gun, for I was the opposite of calm. But I thought for a moment. The pellets might only annoy him, and that might have been the end of me. Taking my rifle, I was about to take aim, when the beast leapt off the rock and was soon hidden in the long grass. We waited for some time, but it did not appear again; for which small mercy I was very thankful.

Putting two and two together, I concluded that this was the beast that must have consumed the dog when we heard the yelp the night before; and we aroused him from his slumbers after his feast. Until I met that lion I thought I was a brave hunter!

Salisbury in these early days was administered by the Chartered Company, and often justice was meted out in a very rough and ready way. The administration of justice to the Mashona was, according to White, beating their pruning-hooks into assegais. His Methodist predecessors had protested and became very unpopular amongst the settlers. A European bully happened to meet White who was dressed in the conventional garb of a missionary. The bully had been reported for his tyranny and was smarting from the exposure. He shouted to White, who was small in stature, ' These damned parsons ought to be kicked out of the country — here is one of them and I've a damned good mind to take it out of him!' White looked at this human hulk steadily and replied, ' I have heard big words from the like of you before now, but they are nothing more than wind.' In the course of his championship of the African White received a good deal of abuse. But he often enjoyed a kindly joke at his own expense, as, for example, the cartoon which ridiculed White as a negrophile or *kaffirboetie* in the local paper. White appeared, a miniature of a man, in his missionary garb, holding a paint-brush in one hand and beside him a pail of distemper. Opposite him was depicted a massive brown figure of an African. The explanatory legend was: ' Don't worry, I'll make you *white*!'

White was no despiser of his fellow-Englishmen; indeed he had such a high admiration for the traditions of justice which they had inherited that he appealed to justice against the current abuses of it. In his later days in Bulawayo it was a deep privilege for him to be more closely associated with the European settlers than was possible in his pioneering missionary days. He was neither uncritically approving of all black-skinned persons, nor irrationally critical of all white skins. The single touchstone for measuring all social attitudes and political policies was brotherhood. He recognized brothers and destroyers of brotherhood, irrespective of pigmentation.

Early in his missionary experience the Mashonaland Rebellion broke out, in 1896. The Mashona most closely identified with his mission at Epworth, not many miles out of Salisbury, became restive and anxious as they heard of the punitive measures planned for the refractory members of their race. They pleaded with their missionary to be included within or near the protective laager established near Salisbury. The Commandant of Salisbury was informed that their loyalty was in doubt and therefore proposed to exclude them from protection. White won the day, however, by protesting, ' If you send these people back to be at the mercy of the rebels, I must go with them '.

The Epworth Mashona, for their part, began to entertain the suspicion that if they went near the laager they would be annihilated by the British. Again, the emissary of the Prince of Peace quietened their fears with the promise, ' I will sleep each night amongst you outside the laager, so that if they come to kill you, they will kill me also '.

During these days John White saw with his own eyes the remarkable loyalty of which the Africans are capable, once the white man has won their trust. The incident deserves to be as well known as the more famous case of Livingstone's carriers bringing his dead body through thousands of swampy and malarial miles to the coast. Molele, a Christian evangelist, of Nengubo, was instructed to bring his family to Epworth Farm or Salisbury for refuge when the rebellion broke out. When preparing to leave, a message came from James White, a European settler, that the rebels had killed his companion and severely wounded him in the leg. The message also asked Molele to come for the settler with a wagon and take him to the Nengubo mission station. Molele knew that to save the life of a white settler (now the enemy of the insurgent Mashona), would be to run the risk of forfeiting his own life as a traitor. Yet he took the fateful but honourable decision. They had only just begun the journey to safety when shots rang out near their wagon. James White urged Molele to make his dash for safety, but he refused to leave the settler. The African evangelist received the full impetus of the first assegai, and the settler fell transfixed by the second. A pathetic remnant of the Molele family which escaped, walked during four nights (hiding during the days) to bring the news to John White in Salisbury. The missionary buried the ashes of the white man and his black friend together beneath a wooden cross.

The missionary's own ashes lie in the same sacred place and the living memorial of this token of racial differences reconciled by the world's Saviour is the great Waddilove Missionary Institution erected in the neighbourhood. It was started in 1898 with a grant of £150 and John White comprised the entire staff. Now it has a fine teacher's training institute, a training school for ministers and evangelists, a lying-in hospital and a new wing for babies. Its impressive buildings have an African structure and appearance and modern scientific amenities. The Methodist Church of Mashonaland is built upon the blood of such a martyr as Molele. If the writer may interject a personal confession of faith here, it was seeing the work of Waddilove, of Hope Fountain and of Cyrene in Southern Rhodesia, that made him believe that in such institutions the most constructive contribution to race relations is made. The most urgent necessity in the greatest human problem in Africa is for trust, and that is unquestionably the fruit of a faith in Christ active in promoting brotherhood. Social integration is possible only on the basis of brotherhood, and brotherhood is achieved by the dissolution of our prejudices and inherited hostilities and fears in the reconciling power of Christ crucified. That was what White preached and practised with such conspicuous success, and that is why his work endures with a finality not given to the demagogues or the economic Communists.

These pioneering years were full of discomforts and perils cheerfully endured. One Christmas Eve, for instance, when he had hoped to reach his headquarters for the festival of the Christ-child which gladdens the home, he had to spend Christmas Eve and Christmas Day in a wagon stuck fast in the mud, in the midst of a small lake that the floods of the night had produced.

What he regularly endured in the way of discomfort may be realized from the following citation from a letter:

> One night we came to a village whose people were unknown to me. We had been on foot since six in the morning and now it was eight o'clock in the evening. You can guess how tired we were! I asked the chief if he could let us have a hut to sleep in and he gave us a small place not more than ten feet across. Five goats were in residence when I retired, and these, an evangelist, four carriers and myself slept together in this awful place! I was glad when dawn came. But should I grumble, when the Son of Man had not where to lay his head?

One of his most fortunate escapes from death occurred when he was prospecting for future missions on the banks of the Zambezi River. He was bending down to treat the injured foot of one of the carriers, and was reaching behind to pull out his clasp-knife, when he caught hold of a deadly snake. Immediately he threw it from him. His dog rushed forward to worry it and received the snake's fangs in its neck. In a short time the dog's head and neck had swollen to double its normal size.

White was not only a pioneer but a first-rate strategist and planner. For most of his missionary life he was the leader of the Methodist Church in the Southern Rhodesia district and this involved directing both European and African work. He had formulated a threefold policy for Christian advance in the Colony. The first priority was the need for the written Word of God to be read and understood in the Shona tongue; the second need was for Native evangelists and teachers as witnesses to Christ; and the third for the integration of the Christian Church with the social life of the Africans. He attempted to meet all three needs, as far as his resources of men, women and

finances would permit. In all three respects he was
astonishingly successful.

The training of evangelists and teachers was undertaken,
as we have seen, at the Waddilove Institution, where for
a time John White was principal and staff. Its predecessor was the Nengubo mission. He was the first translator
of the Scriptures into Shona; indeed, before he came, the
language had not even been reduced to a written ortho-
graphy. Moffat Gautry describes vividly how White
set to work in 1894 to translate St. Mark's Gospel, with
the assistance of his wagon-driver and interpreter, James
Chiremba Chihota:

> A packing-case formed his table, a soap-box his seat, and a
> fruit-tin his writing-pad planted between his Greek New
> Testament and an English Revised Version. Then, with his
> wagon-driver to help him with his vocabulary, he began the
> laborious task of translating those wonderful words of life
> and putting into the Mashona language the Stories of Jesus.

He believed that the Christian way of life must be
integrated into the African social system, and he became
famous for his pioneer experiment at Epworth farm,
near Chiremba's Kraal, where Christian African families
were settled on a co-operative basis and encouraged to
build up a communal religious and social life.

Perhaps the most romantic story of his life concerns
the pushing of the frontiers of the Gospel to the Zambezi.
It began with the son of a chieftain in the Luano valley,
200 miles north of the great river. He had been
converted in a Methodist Church attached to a Rhodesian
mining compound and, returning home, told his father
about the missionaries and their Gospel. His father urged
him to return to Rhodesia and to bring back a missionary
with him. Before he could start, the old chief died and
the younger man had to assume his father's duties. Some
months later the young chief undertook the 350-mile
journey to Epworth on foot. White was deeply impressed

with his sincerity and promised Chikara that he would follow him in a few weeks time to consider the establishment of a mission amongst the chief's people.

White entrained to the rail terminus in Northern Rhodesia and walked the rest of the way. On reaching the kraal they learned that Chikara had been trampled to death a few weeks before by an elephant — they had arrived in time for the mourning ceremonies. The new chief Mbosha seemed friendly and repeated the wish of his predecessor for a missionary to settle among them. John White thought that the presence of the entire clan at the mourning-ceremonies offered an opportunity to be grasped with both hands. He took it. He addressed the assembled tribe, telling them that their former chief Chikara possessed knowledge that he wished to pass on to them, and that this revelation was in the keeping of the missionaries who would gladly transmit it. What impressed White most of all was the fact that the new chief, who was the veriest of babes in Christ, offered a simple extemporaneous prayer at the conclusion of the tribal meeting.

White promised to select a central place for a site for a mission and to send them teachers. The chief said, as the missionary prepared to return, ' Leave part of your luggage behind, so that when I look upon it I may know that you are returning '. Here was a deep hunger for God without parallel in White's experience. The first missionary to the Luano valley, who implemented White's assurances, was J. H. Loveless, a gracious and gallant man.

During the first World War, White's health broke and he had to return to England for treatment. On his return he was forced to take up a less physically exacting task, so he was transferred to Bulawayo. This was essentially industrial work, as his previous labours had been amongst an agrarian community. Here he felt it to be his paramount duty to act as peace-maker between European and African Christians, for there was friction between these two groups: the Europeans seemed apathetic towards the Africans, and the Africans resentful. He was not a little disturbed to find that the Churches themselves had weakened their witness in the face of racial and colour prejudice, and this he fought with all his might. In these years he showed an almost reckless daring: he was one of God's noblest works — a colourblind Christian!

In these years both he and his friend, Arthur Shearly Cripps, were accused of being political meddlers. His invariable reply was that ministers needs not meddle in countries where a political democracy has been built up, but that the situation in Africa was entirely different. Here the missionary has to prove his friendship for the exploited by being identified with their interests, especially as the African is largely voiceless, voteless and defenceless. Furthermore, he was convinced that so-called European Christians (and all white men were assumed by the Africans to be Christians) were betraying the Christian faith by social injustice.

I think that he would have made his own the insight of A. S. Cripps that for a Christian to exploit an African is to exploit Christ. 'In as much as ye have done it unto the least of these my brethren', said Jesus, ' ye have done it unto Me '. Similarly to rebuff an African was to rebuff Christ. Cripps expressed it movingly in his noble poem, the ' Black Christ ':

> To me, as one born out of his due time
> To me, as one not much to reckon in,
> He hath revealed Himself, not as to Paul,
> Christ throned and crowned,
> But marred, despised, rejected,
> The Divine Outcast of a terrible land,
> The Black Christ, with parched lips and empty hand.

His love for the African was deep to the point of sacrifice, but it was not blind love. He loved to tell stories of the incongruities in the African temperament. At one service of marriage he conducted, the first hymn chosen was ' When the storms of life are over'! He suggested that the next hymn should be more cheerful and the choice fell on ' John Brown's body lies a-mouldering in the ground . . .'. On another occasion he had to reprimand a young African at Waddilove for sending simultaneous love-letters to two young girls. The unperturbed wooer replied, ' Yes, minister, but when a man plants his corn, he never knows where the seed will turn up'.

The rest of his life does not make cheerful reading, for it records the progress of the fatal internal disease which held him in an increasingly painful grip. On the diagnosis of Dr. Godfrey Huggins (now the Prime Minister of Southern Rhodesia) he went back to England for an operation, but it was too late, as his first specialist had feared. He and his stout-hearted wife went to live in Kingsmead Close, one of the excellent missionary, educational and ecumenical Colleges of Selly Oak, to the south of Birmingham. Here he was courageous to the end and exercised a veritable ministry in his bedroom, proving that the faith could hold in pain. This episode of his life has been immortalized in C. F. Andrews's fine book, *With Christ in the Silence*. His splendid life on earth ended in 1933, but he will be remembered as long as Christian gallantry and chivalry are honoured.

A SELECT BIBLIOGRAPHY

ANDREWS, C. F. *John White of Mashonaland.* (Hodder & Stoughton. London. 1935.)

ANON. *Mother Cecile in South Africa,* 1883-1906. (S.P.C.K. London. 1930.)

BRABANT, F. H. *Neville Stuart Talbot,* 1879-1943. (S.C.M. Press. London. 1949.)

BROOKE, A. *Robert Gray, First Bishop of Cape Town.* (O.U.P. Cape Town. 1947.)

CASALIS, E. *Mes Souvenirs.* (Librairie Fischbacher. Paris. 1884.)

CLINTON, D. K. *The South African Melting Pot.* (Longmans Green. London. 1937.)

COUVE, D. *Des Monts du Lessouto aux Plaines de Zambèze.* (Société des Missions Evangeliques. Paris. 1926.)

DU PLESSIS, J. *History of Christian Missions in South Africa.* (Longmans Green. London. 1911.)

DU PLESSIS, J. *The Life of Andrew Murray.* (Marshall Bros. London. n.d.)

DU TOIT, S. *Handleiding vir die Studie van die Kerkgeskiedenis.* (Calvyn-Jubileum-Boekefonds. Nasionale Pers. Cape Town. 2nd edition. 1945.)

DU TOIT, S. Article in *Kultuurgeskiedenis van die Afrikaner.* Vol. ii. (Nasionale Pers. Cape Town. 1947.)

GERDENER, G. B. A. *Boustowwe vir die Geskiedenis van die Nederduits-Gereformeerde Kerk in die Transgariep.* (Nasionale Pers. Cape Town. 1930.)

GERDENER, G. B. A. *Studies in the Evangelisation of South Africa.* (Longmans Green. London. 1911.)

GOIRAN, H. *Une Action Créatrice de la Mission Française.* (Éditions Je Sers. Paris. 1931.)

GROVES, C. P. *The Planting of Christianity in Africa.* Vol. i. (Lutterworth Press. London. 1948.)

HARRIS, J. C. *Khama, the Great African Chief.* (Livingstone Press. London. 3rd edition. 1923.)

HEPBURN, J. D. (edited Lyall, C. H.) *Twenty Years in Khama's Country.* (Hodder & Stoughton. London. 1895.)

HOFFMAN, B. *The Founder of Marianhill.* (Marianhill Mission Press. Natal. 1948.)

HOFMEYR, J. W. L. *Die Lewe van Stefanus Hofmeyr, eerste Afrikaanse buitelandse Sendeling.* (1932.)

HOFMEYR, S. *Twintig Jaren in de Zoutpansbergen.* (J. H. Rose. Cape Town. 1890.)

JUNOD, H. A. *Ernest Creux et Paul Berthoud, Les fondateurs de la Mission Suisse dans l'Afrique du Sud.* (Mission Suisse. Lausanne. 1933.)

LAGDEN, G. *The Basutos.* Vols. i, ii. (Hutchinson. London. 1909.)

LATOURETTE, K. S. *History of the Expansion of Christianity.* Vols. v, vii. (Eyre & Spottiswoode. London. 1947.)

LEWIS, C. and EDWARDS, G. E. *Historical Records of the Church of the Province of South Africa.* (S.P.C.K. London. 1934.)

LIVINGSTONE, D. *Missionary Travels and Researches in South Africa.* (Harper & Bros. New York. 1858.)

LOVETT, R. *History of the London Missionary Society.* Vol. i. (Henry Frowde. London. 1899.)

MACKENZIE, J. *Ten Years North of the Orange River.* (Edmonston & Douglas. Edinburgh. 1871.)

MACKINTOSH, C. W. *Coillard of the Zambezi.* (London. 1907.)

MACMILLAN, W. M. *The Cape Colour Question.* (Faber & Gwyer. London. 1927.)

MACNAIR, J. I. *Livingstone the Liberator.* (Collins. London. n.d.)

MARTIN, A. D. *Doctor Vanderkemp.* (Livingstone Press. London. n.d.)

MOFFAT, J. S. *The Lives of Robert and Mary Moffat.* (T. Fisher Unwin. London. 1885.)

MOFFAT, R. *Missionary Labours and Scenes in Southern Africa.* (John Snow. London. 1842.)

MOOREES, A. *Die Nederduitse Gereformeerde Kerk in Suid Afrika, 1652-1873.* (S.A. Bybelvereeniging. Cape Town. 1937.)

NIENABER, P. J. *Jan Lion Cachet met sy Sewe Duiwels.* (J. L. van Schaik. Pretoria. 1940.)

PAGE, B. T. *The Harvest of Good Hope.* (Centenary History of the Church of the Province.) (S.P.C.K. London. 1947.)

PHILIP, J. *Researches in South Africa.* Vols. i, ii. (James Duncan. London. 1828.)

ROBINS, M. W. *Mother Cecile of Grahamstown, South Africa.* (Wells, Gardner & Darton. London. 1939.)

SCHIMLEK, F. *Against the Stream.* (Biography of Father Bernard Huss.) (Marianhill Mission Press. Natal. 1949.)

SCHIMLEK, F. *Medicine versus Witchcraft.* (Marianhill Mission Press. Natal. 1950.)

SHAW, W. *The Story of my Mission in South-Eastern Africa.* (Hamilton Adams. London. 1860.)

SHEPHERD, R. H. W. *Lovedale, South Africa, 1841-1941.* (Lovedale Press. Lovedale. n.d.)

SHEPHERD, R. H. W. *Where Aloes Flame.* (Lutterworth Press. London. 1948.)

SHILLITO, E. *François Coillard, a Wayfaring Man.* (S.C.M. Press. London. 1923.)

SMITH, E. W. *The Life and Times of Daniel Lindley, 1801-1890.* (Epworth Press. London. 1949.)

SMITH, E. W. *Robert Moffat, one of God's Gardeners.* (S.C.M. Press. London. 1925.)

SOUTHON, A. E. *Khama the Conqueror.* (Atlantis Press. London. n.d.)

WELLS, J. *Stewart of Lovedale.* (Hodder & Stoughton. London. 1909. 2nd edition 1919.)

WHITESIDE, J. *History of the Wesleyan Methodist Church of South Africa.* (Elliot Stock. London. 1906.)

INDEX

183